JEWISH MYSTICISM

An Introduction to the Kabbalah

J. Abelson

DOVER PUBLICATIONS, INC.
Mineola, New York

Published in Canada by General Publishing Company, Ltd., 895 Don Mills Road, 400-2 Park Centre, Toronto, Ontario M3C 1W3.
Published in the United Kingdom by David & Charles, Brunel House, Forde Close, Newton Abbot, Devon TQ12 4PU.

Bibliographical Note

This Dover edition, first published in 2001, is an unabridged republication of the work originally published in 1913 under the title *Jewish Mysticism* by G. Bell and Sons Ltd., London.

Library of Congress Cataloging-in-Publication Data

Abelson, J. (Joshua), 1873–1940.
    Jewish mysticism : an introduction to the Kabbalah / J. Abelson.
        p. cm.
    Originally published: London : G. Bell and Sons, 1913.
    Includes bibliographical references.
    ISBN 0-486-41996-7 (pbk.)
        1. Mysticism—Judaism. 2. Cabala. I. Title.

BM723 .A2 2001
296.1'6—dc21

2001032489

Manufactured in the United States of America
Dover Publications, Inc., 31 East 2nd Street, Mineola, N.Y. 11501

EDITOR'S PREFACE

GENERAL and special studies on Christian
mysticism are numerous enough; but it is
somewhat remarkable that, in their introductory pages, authors, who have much
to say of Plotinus and Neoplatonism, have
nothing or very little on the still more
cognate subject of Jewish mysticism. This
is not, however, so very surprising, for,
truth to tell, there is a singular dearth of
anything like an adequate introduction to
the study of Jewish mysticism itself. The
impression left with the general reader is
that there is little of a mystical nature
in the legitimate tradition of Jewish religion, and that the Kabbalah is simply a
morbid and late growth, fed entirely by
elements foreign to the genius of Israel.
How ill-founded is the former view, and
how extreme the latter, may be seen in the
following pages. In an able summary, that

may well serve as an introduction to the general study of Jewish mysticism, Dr. Abelson makes accessible to the general reader, in simple terms, the results of his careful inquiry, based on the researches of the best Jewish scholars, and reinforced by his own wide acquaintance with Talmudic and Rabbinical literature. To write profitably on Jewish mysticism, it is necessary to have, not only a discriminating sympathy with the mystical standpoint, but also a first-hand knowledge of Jewish religious literature, the peculiar genius of which, perhaps, no one but a member of the race that has produced it can adequately appreciate and interpret. In addition to this, Dr. Abelson comes well prepared for his task, as he has already opened up a new field of research by his valuable critical study on *The Immanence of God in Rabbinical Literature*, a subject which is the indispensable presupposition of all Jewish mysticism.

PREFACE

THE following pages are designed to give the reader a bird's-eye view of the salient features in Jewish mysticism rather than a solid presentation of the subject as a whole. The reason for this will be apparent when one thinks of the many centuries of variegated thought that have had to be packed within the small number of pages allotted to the book. It is this very fact, too, that will possibly give the present treatment of the subject a fragmentary and tentative appearance. Thus Chapter V. follows immediately upon the contents of Chapter IV., without the least attempt to show any of the numerous intervening stages of development. Similarly, Chapter VI., dealing with the *Zohar*, should have been preceded by an exposition of the evolution of Jewish theological thought in the many centuries which divide that chapter from the matter contained in the

previous chapter.   But lack of space made
these omissions inevitable. Should the reader
be stimulated to a deeper study of the
subject, he will be easily led to the missing
parts by the aid of the bibliography at the
end of the book.

I should add that the translated extracts
from the *Zohar* are only in some cases made
by me from the original Hebrew-Aramaic.   I
owe many of them to the French and German
translations to be found in the works of the
scholars from whom I have drawn much of
my material.

J. ABELSON.

Aria College, Portsmouth.

CONTENTS

JEWISH MYSTICISM

INTRODUCTION

It might strike the average reader as exceedingly odd that any attempt should be made at writing a book on Jewish mysticism. The prevailing opinion—among theologians as well as in the mind of the ordinary man—seems to be that Judaism and mysticism stand at the opposite poles of thought, and that, therefore, such a phrase as Jewish mysticism is a glaring and indefensible contradiction in terms. It is to be hoped that the contents of this little book will show the utter falsity of this view.

What is this view, in the main, based upon? It is based upon the gratuitous assumption that the Old Testament, and all the theological and religious literature produced by Jews in subsequent ages, as well as the general synagogue ritual, the public and private religious worship of the Jew—that all these are grounded on the unquestioning assumption of an *exclusively transcendent God*. The Jews, it is said, never got any

higher than the notion of the old Jehovah
whose abode was in the highest of the seven
heavens and whose existence, although very
very real to the Jew, was yet of a kind so
immeasurably far away from the scenes of
earth that it could not possibly have that
significance for the Jew which the God of
Christianity has for the Christian. The Jew,
it is said, could not possibly have that inward
experience of God which was made possible
to the Christian by the life of Jesus and the
teaching of Paul.

This is one erroneous assumption. A
second is the following : The Pauline anti-
thesis of law and faith has falsely stamped
Judaism as a religion of unrelieved legalism ;
and mysticism is the irreconcileable enemy
of legalism. The God of the Jew, it is said,
is a lawgiver pure and simple. The loyal
and conscientious Jew is he who lives in the
throes of an uninterrupted obedience to a
string of laws which hedge him round on all
sides. Religion is thus a mere outward
mechanical and burdensome routine. It is
one long bondage to a Master whom no one
has at any time seen or experienced. All
spirituality is wanting. God is, as it were, a
fixture, static. He never goes out of His
impenetrable isolation. Hence He can have
no bond of union with any one here below.
Hence, further, He must be a stranger to the
idea of Love. There can be no such thing as

a self-manifestation of a loving God, no movement of the Divine Spirit towards the human spirit and no return movement of the human spirit to the Divine Spirit. There can be no fellowship with God, no opportunity for any immediate experiences by which the human soul comes to partake of God, no incoming of God into human life. And where there is none of these, there can be no mystical element.

A third false factor in the judgment of Christian theologians upon Judaism is their insistence upon the fact that the intense and uncompromising national character of Judaism must of necessity be fatal to the mystical temperament. Mystical religion does, of course, transcend all the barriers which separate race from race and religion from religion. The mystic is a cosmopolitan, and, to him, the differences between the demands and beliefs and observances of one creed and those of another are entirely obliterated in his one all-absorbing and all-overshadowing passion for union with Reality. It is therefore quite true that if Judaism demands of its devotees that they should shut up their God in one sequestered, watertight compartment, it cannot at the same time be favourable to the quest pursued by the mystic.

But as against this, it must be urged that Judaism in its evolution through the cen-

turies has not been so hopelessly particularist
as is customarily imagined. The message
of the Old Testament on this head must be
judged by the condition of things prevailing
in the long epoch of its composition. The
message of the Rabbinical literature and of
much of the Jewish mediæval literature must
similarly be judged. The Jew was the butt
of the world's scorn. He was outcast, de-
graded, incapacitated, denied ever so many
of the innocent joys and advantages which
are the rightful heritage of all the children of
men, no matter what their distinctive race
or creed might be. He retaliated by de-
claring (as a result of conviction), in his
literature and in his liturgy, that his God
could not, by any chance, be the God of the
authors of all these acts of wickedness and
treachery. Idolatry, immorality, impurity,
murder, persecution, hatred—the workers of
all these must perforce be shut out from the
Divine presence. Hence seeing that, in the
sight of the Jew, the nations were the personification of these detestable vices, and
seeing that the Jew, in all the pride of a long
tradition, looked upon himself as invested
with a spirit of especial sanctity, as entrusted
with the mission of a holy and pure priest-
hood, one can quite easily understand how
he came to regard the God of Truth and
Mercy as first and foremost his God and no
one else's.

But with all this, there are, in all branches of Jewish literature, gleams of a far wider, more tolerant, and universalist outlook. Instances will be quoted later. The fact that they existed shows that the germs of the universalism implied in mysticism were there, only they were crushed by the dead-weight of a perverse worldly fate. The Jew certainly did, and could, find God in his neighbour (a non-Jew) as well as in himself. And this ability is, and always was, a strong point of the mystics. Further, even if it be granted that there are in Judaism elements of a nationalism which can hardly be made to square with a high spirituality, this is no necessary bar to its possession of abiding and deeply-ingrained mystical elements. Nationalism is an integral and vital part of the Judaism of the Old Testament and the Rabbinical literature. It is bone of its bone, spirit of its spirit. It is so interfused with religion that it is itself religion. You cannot take up the old Judaism and break it up into pieces, saying : Here are its religious elements ; there are its national elements. The two are inextricably combined, warp and woof of one texture. And thus it came about that—strange as it may appear to the modern mind—a halo of religious worth and of strong spirituality was thrown over beliefs and practices which, considered in and for themselves, are nothing more than national

sentiments, national memories, and national
aspirations.   Such, then, being the case, the
relation of Judaism to Jewish nationalism is
the relation of a large circle to the smaller
circle inscribed within it.   The larger em-
braces the smaller.

To come now to mysticism ; the mystic
differs from the ordinary religionist in that
whereas the latter knows God through an
objective revelation whether in nature or as
embodied in the Bible (which is really only
second-hand knowledge, mediate, external,
the record of other people's visions and
experiences), the mystic knows God by contact of spirit with spirit ; *cor ad cor
loquitur.* He has the immediate vision ; he
hears the still small voice speaking clearly
to him in the silence of his soul.   In this sense
the mystic stands quite outside the field of
all the great religions of the world.   Religion
for him is merely *his own* individual religion,
his own lonely, isolated quest for truth.   He
is solitary—a soul alone with God.

But when we examine the lives and works
of mystics, what do we usually find ?   We
usually find that in spite of the intensely
individualistic type of their religion, they are
allied with some one particular religion of the
world's religions.   Their mystical experiences
are coloured and moulded by *some one*
dominant faith.   The specific forms of their
conceptions of God do not come from their

own inner light only, but from the teachings which they imbibe from the external and traditional religion of their race or country. Thus, Christian mysticism has characteristics which are *sui generis*; so has Mohammedan mysticism; so has Hindu mysticism; and likewise Jewish mysticism. The method, the temperament, the spirit are very much the same in all of them. But the influence wielded over them by the nature and trend of each of the great dominant religions is a decisive one, and stamps its features on them in a degree which makes them most easily distinguishable from one another. Thus Judaism, whatever be its composition or spiritual outlook, can certainly be a religion of mysticism. Its mysticism may be of a different order from that which we commonly expect. But this we shall see into later.

I have thus far dealt with the misconstructions put upon Judaism and its mysticism by theologians outside the Jewish fold. I must now say something about the erroneous judgments passed upon the subject by some Jewish theologians. Jewish mysticism is as old as the Old Testament—nay, as old as some of the oldest parts of the Old Testament. It prevailed in varying degrees of intensity throughout the centuries comprised in the Old Testament history. The current flowed on, uninterrupted, into the era covered by the Rabbinic period. The religious and

philosophical literature, ritual, worship, of
Jewish mediævalism became heirs to it,
developing and ramifying its teachings and
implications in ways which it is the purport
of this book partially to tell.

Now, more than one Jewish writer has
categorically asserted that the origins of
Jewish mysticism date back not, as is the
fact, to the mists of antiquity, but to the
period of European-Jewish history beginning
with the 12th century. The German-Jewish
historian, H. Graetz (1817–1891), one of the
best-known upholders of this view, ascribes
the origin of Jewish mysticism to a French
Rabbi of the 12th and 13th centuries, by
name Isaac ben Abraham of Posquières,
more generally known as Isaac the Blind.
He regards him as the father ' of the Kabbalah '—the latter term being the general
name in Jewish literature for every kind or
school of mystical interpretation. Isaac is
the reputed author of the Hebrew mystical
treatise written in dialogue form and called
Bahir (' Brightness ')—the book which, more
than all its predecessors in this domain, anticipates the style and contents of the *Zohar*
(' Shining '), which is *par excellence* the
mediæval text-book of Jewish mysticism,
and belongs to the 14th century. Graetz
regards the appearance of this mysticism as
some sudden, unexplained importation from
without, a plant of exotic origin, " a false

doctrine which, although new, styled itself a primitive inspiration ; although un-Jewish, called itself a genuine teaching of Israel " (*History of the Jews,* English Trans., vol. iii. p. 565).

But a perusal of the Old Testament, the New Testament (much of which is Hebraic in thought and the work of Jews), and the Rabbinic records will not, for one moment, lend countenance to such a theory. It is in these early monuments of Judaism that the origins will be found. Of course, in saying that the Old Testament holds elements of mysticism—and in saying the same thing of the New Testament—it must be understood that the mysticism is of an implicit and unconscious kind and not the type of religion historically known as ' mysticism.' It is ever so far removed from the mysticism of a Plotinus or an Eckhart or an Isaac Luria (Jewish mystic, 1533–1572). But taking mysticism in its broader connotation as meaning religion in its most acute, intense, and living stage (Rufus Jones, *Studies in Mystical Religion,* p. xv.), an immediate and first-hand experience of God, then the ascription of mysticism to the Old and New Testaments is perfectly correct. And, as will be obvious from our coming pages, the most highly-elaborated mystical doctrines of Jews in all ages subsequent to the Old Testament are, after allowing for certain extraneous

additions, an offshoot of the latter's teachings.

Another type of ill-considered and unjust
judgment often passed on Jewish mysticism
by Jewish authorities, is to be found in the
sneering and condemnatory attitude they
adopt towards it in their writings. This,
of course, is a phenomenon by no means
confined to Jews. One need only think of
the hostility of men like Ritschl, Nordau,
and Harnack towards all mysticism, indiscriminately. The antagonism springs, in
all cases, from an inability to appreciate
the subjectivity and individualism of the
mystical temperament. While rationalism
attempts to solve the ultimate problems of
existence by the application of the intellect
and the imagination, mysticism takes account
of the cravings of the heart and of the great
fact of the soul. Pure philosophy will never
avail to give the final answer to the questions, '' what is above, what is below, what
is in front, what is behind '' (Mishna,
Ḥaggigah, ii. 1). The world, to man's pure
intellect, consists only of that which is seen
and which is temporal. But there is another world transcending it, a world invisible, incomprehensible, but yet both
visible and comprehensible to the soul's
craving for communion with the Divine.
No ratiocination, no syllogism of logic, can
strip off the veil from this elusive world.

The pathway to it lies through something quite other than intellectuality or sense-experience. It can be grasped only by those inward indefinable movements of feeling or emotion which, in their totality, constitute the soul.

From all this it follows that scholars who, whether congenitally or by mental training, have no sympathy with the subjectivity of the emotions, should be incapable of appreciating the paraphernalia of mysticism.

But in the case of Jewish theologians there is something more to be said. As will be seen in the course of our coming pages, mystical speculation among the Jews clustered largely round the cosmological sections of the Bible. This is true of the earlier as well as of the later mysticism. It is to be found in the Enoch literature, a product of the first pre-Christian century (see Charles, *The Book of the Secrets of Enoch*, 1896, p. xxv.), as well as in the Kabbalistic works produced in France, Spain, Germany, and Poland from the 12th to the 18th century. Combined with this cosmological speculation— or rather as an outcome of it—there went an anthropomorphism which cannot be described otherwise than as being gross. And, in addition to this, a mysterious power was ascribed to the permutations and combinations of the letters of the Hebrew alphabet. By some of the most extraordinary feats of verbal jugglery these letters are made to prove all sorts of things in heaven and earth. They are purely fantastic, and no one can possibly take them seriously. The treatment of the question of the soul, too, gave rise to many curious beliefs about the transmigration of the soul and the appearance of the soul of the Messiah.

All these aspects of Jewish mysticism, tainted as they undoubtedly are by many unlovely characteristics, have been eagerly seized upon by the critics in order to show the unedifying nature of the whole teaching. But it is really an unfair criticism, seeing that it leaves totally out of account the preponderating mass of true poetry and spirituality which inhere in all parts of Jewish mystical speculation. We shall have occasion to give many illustrations of this statement in pages to follow. Nowhere in Jewish literature is the idea of prayer raised to such a pitch of sublimity as it is in the lives and writings of the Jewish mystics. If it is true to say that Judaism here and there suffers from too large an element of formalism and legalism and externalism, it is equally true to say that many of these drawbacks are corrected, toned down, by the contributions of mysticism. And although its treatment of the soul is in many ways overwrought and far-fetched, it is good to know that there is a side of Judaism which laid stress not only on the importance of our securing happiness or reward in this earthly life but also in the life beyond. Jewish mysticism can congratulate itself in having, at one momentous epoch of Jewish history, achieved for Judaism a boon, which Christian mysticism in quite another way, but in an equally important degree, achieved for Christianity. Systematic Christian mysticism began in the late 14th and early 15th centuries. Its foremost exponent was Meister Eckhart, the Dominican monk. What Eckhart and his followers achieved may be summarised by saying that they relieved Christendom of the heavy load of arid scholasticism under which it had for long been oppressed, and, by introducing ideas of religion at once more simple, more practical, more social, and more spiritual, paved the way for the New Learning — for the new discoveries in science and philosophy which were to revolutionise the world. In other words, this Christian mysticism was the avenue through which the subtle dark speculations of an Albertus Magnus and a Thomas Aquinas had necessarily to pass in order to prepare coming ages for the light of a Newton, a Kant, and a Darwin. Hence must modern science come down from the pedestal of her pomp and glory, and bow her acknow-

ledgments to the services of many a humble
Christian mystic.

Jewish mysticism has a similar act of
homage to receive at the hands of every
lover of Jewish scholarship. In the 13th
century Judaism was in danger of becoming
devitalised through the theology of Moses
Maimonides—the great Spanish-Jewish theologian and author of the famous *Guide
of the Perplexed*—who looked upon reason
as the final arbiter of the rightness or
wrongness of any Jewish dogma. Judaism
for him was a cult of the intellect and the
intellect only. The sole representative of
the intellect was Aristotle. Nearly everything in Judaism had by hook or by crook
to be harmonised with the tenets of
Aristotelianism. Thus, Jewish morality
must, to have validity, be shown to be in
consonance with Aristotle's four faculties
of the soul and with his theories of ' the
mean.' Judaism's teachings on the unity
of God must be brought into line with the
Aristotelian indivisible God, who is the
principal of all essences, the disposer of
the world. Just as intellectual perfection
is, to the Greek philosopher, the highest aim
of man, so must the teachings of Judaism
be interpreted in such a way as to show
that, according to the Torah, the life of the
saint is a life of the highest intellectuality.
Revelation—which is one of the corner-

stones of the Jewish faith—must be in accordance with reason. All the truths enunciated by Plato and Aristotle are anticipated in the writings of the Prophets and of some of the Talmudic sages. The prophets, according to Maimonides, were the recipients, orally, of a set of philosophical doctrines which were handed on orally from father to son, from generation to generation, until the age of the Talmud. Philosophy is an echo of them. What a fossilising, deteriorating effect the spread of these teachings must have wielded upon Judaism had they been allowed to go on without check !

The check came in the shape of mysticism. It corrected the balance. It showed that Judaism was a religion of the *feelings* as well as of the intellect. It showed that the Jew's eternal quest was not to be right with Aristotle but to be right with God. It showed that Judaism has a place not only for Reason but for Love too. It showed that the ideal life of the Jew was, not a life of outward harmony with rules and prescriptions, but a life of inward attachment to a Divine Life which is immanent everywhere, and that the crown and consummation of all effort consists in finding a direct way to the actual presence of God.

CHAPTER I

SOME EARLY ELEMENTS : ESSENISM

THE Old Testament is the fountain-head of Judaism. Hence if it is true, as is contended in a previous page, that the Old Testament contains mystical elements, then the starting-point in any treatment of Jewish mysticism on historical, or even semi-historical, lines must be the Old Testament. But this course will not be adopted here. The Old Testament will be omitted. And for a reason which has already been hinted. The mysticism of the Old Testament is of an elementary, naïve, and unconscious kind, whereas what this book is intended to show is the consciously-elaborated, professional mysticism of the Jews. What we get in the Old Testament are the ground-work and the scaffolding, the indispensable beginnings of the edifice ; but not the edifice itself.

Thus it has much to say about the Father-hood of God. Here we have a basic conception of all mysticism ; for the latter in all its phases and stages assumes the possibility of communion with some one who, while greater and more powerful than ourselves, is at the same time loving, and benevolent, and personally interested in us. You can only pray to one who hears; you can only feel love towards one who, you know, has loved you first. The Old Testament scintillates with sublime examples of men whose communion with God was a thing of intensest reality to them, and whose conviction of the ' nearness ' of the Divine was beyond the slightest cavil. The sudden and unexpected inrushes of Divine inspiration which seized the Old Testament prophets; Isaiah's vision of a God ' whose train filled the Temple '—an emblem of the All-inclusiveness of Deity, of the presence and the working of an all-embracing Spirit of Life; the ecstasy of an Ezekiel lifted from off his feet by the Spirit and removed from one place to another; the fact of prophecy itself—the possession of a spiritual endowment not vouchsafed to ordinary men, the endowment of a higher insight into the will of God;—all these represent a stage of first-hand, living religion to which the name of mysticism is rightly and properly applied. But they are no more than the preamble to the explicit, conscious, and pronouncedly personal type of Jewish mysticism which is the subject of the present book.

The earliest beginnings of this mysticism are usually accredited, by modern Jewish scholars, to the Essenes. To say this, is to put back Jewish mysticism to a very early date, for according to the theory of Wellhausen (*Israëlitische und jüdische Geschichte*, 1894, p. 261), the Essenes as well as the Pharisees were offshoots of the Ḥasidim (חסידים = 'pious ones') of the pre-Maccabean age. But it is only a theory, and not an established historical fact, seeing that the religious tenets of the Jews during the three centuries immediately preceding the birth of Christianity are veiled in considerable obscurity, and seeing also that the real meaning of the name 'Essenes' as well as their exact relations with the Pharisees are points upon which there is anything but certainty. What is certain, however, is that three outstanding literary sources belonging to the first two or three Christian centuries—viz. (*a*) Philo, (*b*) Josephus, (*c*) some older portions of the Babylonian and Palestinian Talmuds—all have stray allusions, couched in varying phraseology, to certain sects or parties who differed in their mode of life from the general body of the Jews, and who were in possession of certain esoteric teachings of which those outside their ranks were uninformed.

Thus Philo (*Quod omnis probus liber*, 12) writes of them that they were " eminently worshippers of God (θεραπευταὶ θεοῦ), not in the sense that they sacrifice living animals (like the priests in the Temple), but that they are anxious to keep their minds in a priestly state of holiness. They prefer to live in villages, and avoid cities on account of the habitual wickedness of those who inhabit them, knowing, as they do, that just as foul air breeds disease, so there is danger of contracting an incurable disease of the soul from such bad associations."

Again, in another of his works (*De Vita contemplativa*, ed. Conybeare, pp. 53, 206), Philo says : " Of natural philosophy . . . they study only that which pertains to the existence of God and the beginning of all things, otherwise they devote all their attention to ethics, using as instructors the laws of their fathers, which, without the outpouring of the Divine Spirit, the human mind could not have devised . . . for, following their ancient traditions, they obtain their philosophy by means of allegorical interpretations. . . . Of the love of God they exhibit myriads of examples, inasmuch as they strive for a continued uninterrupted life of purity and holiness ; they avoid swearing and falsehood, and they declare that God causes only good and no evil whatsoever. . . . No one possesses a house absolutely as his own, one which does not at the same time belong to all; for, in addition to living together in companies, their houses are open also to their adherents coming from other

quarters. They have one storehouse for all,
and the same diet ; their garments belong to
all in common, and their meals are taken in
common."

Josephus speaks of the Essenes in similar
terms (see *Antiquities*, XVIII. i. 2–6 ; also
De Bello Judaico, II. viii. 2–13).

The points to be noted in both the fore-
mentioned authors are : (*a*) the great stress
laid on fellowship, amounting to a kind of
communism ; (*b*) their removal from the
general people by reason of their higher
sanctity ; (*c*) their devotion to the knowledge of the existence of God and the beginning of all things ; (*d*) their love of allegorical interpretation.

Although it is exceedingly difficult to know
what the Rabbinic term equivalent to ' Ess-
ene ' is, it is not hard to deduce, from names
and phrases scattered throughout the Rabbinic
records, a theory that there existed as early
as the first Christian centuries either a distinct
sect of Jews, or individual Jews here and
there, who combined mystical speculation
with an ascetic mode of life.

A similar phenomenon is observable in
the history of the early Christian Church.
There was a life of primitive and austere
fellowship. A group here, a group there,
gathered together with no other motive than
that of gaining a greater hold on the spiritual
life than was prevalent in the ordinary circles

of the people: " And the multitude of them
that believed were of one heart and soul;
and not one of them said that aught of the
things which he possessed was his own; but
they had all things common. . . . For
neither were there among them any that
lacked: for as many as were possessors of
lands or houses sold them . . . and distribution was made unto each according as
any one had need " (*Acts*, iv. 32–35).

They seem to have lived on the border-
land of an unusual ecstasy, experiencing
extraordinary invasions of the Divine, hearing mystic sounds and seeing mystic visions
which, to them, were the direct and immediate
revelations of the deepest and most sacred
truths.

Illustrations of similar experiences in the
bosom of the early synagogue, as presented in
the Rabbinic records, are the following:

There are several heterogeneous passages
which speak of the existence within the
ancient Temple at Jerusalem of a special
apartment, called the *lishkât ḥashāïm*
('chamber of the silent [or secret] ones ').
According to the statement of *Tosefta
Shekalim*, ii. 16, there were to be found in
some cities of Palestine and Babylon men
known as *Ḥashāïm*, who reserved a special
room in their house for depositing in it a
charity-box into which money for the poor
could be put and withdrawn with the utmost

silence. It was collected and distributed by men appointed for the purpose by the *Ḥashāīm*, and, as it was all done with the strictest secrecy, it looks as though there was a kind of communism among the members of the order. The special chamber in the Temple, as mentioned above, was also a place where gifts for the poor were deposited in secret and withdrawn for distribution in secret.

Two facts seem to demonstrate that these *Ḥashāīm* were a small mystical sect.

Firstly, they are given the special appellation of *yirē-ḥēt*, *i.e.* 'fearers of sin.' They were thus marked off by an extra sanctity from the body of the people—and the student of the Rabbinic literature knows that whenever a special title is accorded to a group or sect on the grounds of special holiness, this holiness is always of an exceptionally high order. It is the holiness of men in touch with the Divine. And, as has just been remarked, their enthusiasm for doing good seems to have been grounded on a kind of austere fellowship that reigned among them, impelling them to do their work unseen by the madding crowd.

Secondly, the idea of silence or secrecy was frequently employed by the early Rabbis in their mystical exegesis of Scripture. A typical illustration is the following passage from the *Midrash Rabba* on *Genesis* iii. :

" R. Simeon son of Jehozedek asked R. Samuel son of Naḥman (two Palestinian teachers of the beginning of the 3rd century A.D.) and said unto him, Seeing that I have heard concerning thee that thou art an adept in the Haggadah,[1] tell me whence the light was created.   He replied, It [*i.e.* the Haggadah] tells us that the Holy One (blessed be He) enwrapped Himself in a garment, and the brightness of His splendour lit up the universe from end to end.   He [*i.e.* the sage who just replied] said this in a *whisper,* upon which the other sage retorted, Why dost thou tell this in a whisper, seeing that it is taught clearly in a scriptural verse—' who coverest thyself with light as with a garment ' ? (*Psalm,* civ. 2).   Just as I have myself had it whispered unto me, replied he, even so have I whispered it unto thee."

Another instance of what looks like a sect of esoteric teachers among the Jews of the first centuries is the *Vatīkīn, i.e.* ' men of firm principles.' Their mysticism seems to have clustered mostly round the sentiments and outward conduct governing prayer. Indeed, throughout Rabbinical literature the true suppliant before God is in many cases a mystic. Only the mystic mood is the true prayerful mood. There is a discussion in the Mishna of *Berachoth,* i. 2, as to what is the

---

[1] Haggadah is the general name for the narrative or fabular or philosophical sections of the Rabbinic literature.

earliest moment in the dawn at which the
Shema' (the technical name for *Deuteronomy*,
vi. 4–9) may be read.   Upon this the comment is made, in *T.B. Berachoth*, 9b, that
" the *Vatīkīn* arranged the time for prayer
in such a way as to enable them to finish the
reading of the Shema' at the exact moment
of sunrise."   According to the great Rabbinic
commentator R. Solomon b. Isaac (11th
century), the *Vatīkīn* were " men who were
meek and carried out the commandment
from pure love."   It must be borne in mind
that throughout Jewish theology, ' meekness ' (*'anavah*) stands for something im-
mensely higher than the moral connotation
which we customarily attribute to the virtue.
It signifies a level of religious devoutness
which it is not given to every one to reach.
To carry out a commandment from pure
love, means, in Jewish theology of all ages,
to attain a high stage of mystic elation which
can only be arrived at as the result of a long
preliminary series of arduous efforts in the
upward path.   To recite the Shema' is, as
the Rabbis frequently say, " to take upon
one's self the yoke of the Kingdom of
Heaven," and the phrase ' Kingdom of
Heaven ' has decidedly mystical associations,
as we shall see later.   Hence one may plaus-
ibly conclude that the *Vatīkīn* were a
brotherhood whose dominant feature was a
simplicity of living combined with a degree

of earnest scrupulousness in prayer amounting to an adoration, a love, of the Divine such as is experienced by the mystics of all nations and all times.

And a similar description might be applied to the members of what apparently was another esoteric order of those days—the *Zenūim, i.e.* 'lowly, chaste ones.' As a matter of fact the Rabbinic records are too vague and disconnected to enable scholars to say with any certainty whether these *Zenūim* were an independent sect or whether the word is merely another term denoting either or both of the other fellowships already alluded to. They bear the hall-mark of all ancient and mediæval Jewish mysticism in respect of the emphasis laid by them on the importance of the letters comprising the Divine Name in Hebrew as well as upon certain manipulations of the Hebrew alphabet generally. The following passage occurs in *T.B. Ḳiddushin,* 71a :

" R. Judah said in the name of Rab [*i.e.* R. Abba Arika, a Babylonian teacher of the 3rd century A.D.] the Name of forty-two letters can only be entrusted by us to him who is modest [*i.e. zenūa*'] and meek, in the midway of life, not easily provoked to anger, temperate, and free from vengeful feelings. He who understands it, is cautious with it and keeps it in purity, is loved above and is liked here below. He is revered by his

he is heir to two worlds—this
e world to come."

resting to quote here the com-
is Rabbinic passage made by the
Hebrew philosopher Moses Maimoni-
–1204) in his great work *The Guide*
rplexed. He says (part i. ch. lxii. Eng.
Trans. by M. Friedlander, Routledge, 1906):

"There was also a name of forty-two letters
known among them. Every intelligent per-
son knows that one word of forty-two letters is
impossible. But it was a phrase of several
words which had together forty-two letters.
There is no doubt that the words had such a
meaning as to convey a correct notion of the
essence of God, in the way we have stated.
. . . Many believe that the forty-two letters
are merely to be pronounced mechanically;
that by the knowledge of these, without any
further interpretation, they can attain to
those exalted ends. . . . On the contrary it
is evident that all this exalted preparation
aims at a knowledge of metaphysics and
includes ideas which constitute ' the secrets
of the Law ' as we have explained."

Maimonides, it should be remembered, was
a rationalist and anti-mystic; and much of
the old Rabbinic cosmological mysticism
which was looked upon as serious mystical
speculation by many of his literary con-
temporaries, was dubbed by him as metaphysics or physics.

But, to return to our subject, the best insight into the origin and implication of these forty-two letters is afforded us by the Talmudic passage last quoted (*T.B. Kiddushin*, 71a), where we are told that in the last days of the Temple the decadent priests were deemed unworthy to pronounce the Divine Name in their official benedictions, and a name consisting of twelve letters was substituted. What this name was is nowhere given in the Rabbinic records. As time went on, it was deemed inadvisable to entrust even this twelve-lettered name to every priest. It was taught only to an elect set among them, who, when chanting the benedictions in the general company of all the priests, used to ' swallow ' its pronunciation (*i.e.* make it inaudible) in order not to divulge it. The forty-two-lettered name probably arose in similar circumstances, but whether the secrets of it were confided to a greater or a smaller circle than that in which the twelve-lettered name was known, is by no means apparent. Let it only be said here—as it is a subject to which we shall return later on—that in the elaborated systems of the mediæval Kabbalists these many-lettered names of God (not only forty-two, but also forty-five and seventy-two letters) are the pivots on which huge masses of most curious mystical lore turn. The Ten Sefirot have close connections with these doctrines of letters—

secret doctrines about the Divine nature,
about creation, about the relations subsisting
between God and the universe.

Reference must here be made to what
appears to be another order of Jewish
mystics in the opening centuries of the
Christian era. The Mishna (Tractate
Sukkah, v. 2) speaks of ' the Ḥasidim and
Anshé Ma'aseh ' (*i.e.* saints and miracle-
workers) who, at the joyous feast of the
water-drawing at the Temple during Taber-
nacles, used to dance and perform certain
acrobatic feats with lighted torches. The
allusions are very vaguely worded, and it is
hazardous to deduce any hard - and - fast
theories. But so much may be said, *viz.*
that being mentioned together in the same
Mishna passage just quoted, and being
mentioned in close succession in another
old passage of the Mishna (Tractate *Soṭah*,
ix. 15), it is more than probable that they
belonged to one and the same sect. Again
the phrase ' Anshé Ma'aseh ' (as well as
the singular form of the first word) is frequently used in Rabbinic to mean ' miracle-
worker,' although in the Biblical Hebrew
it would signify ' man of action.' There
is a passage in *T.B. Berachoth*, 18b, which
gives a weird description of the experience
of a ' Ḥasid ' who heard ' from behind the
curtain ' certain secrets hidden from ordinary
men. And the student of Rabbinics knows

how many a Rabbi of these early centuries,
gifted with the mystic temperament, wielded
a semi-miraculous power of foretelling the
future or of creating something out of
nothing (see on this, Volz's *Der Geist Gottes*,
Tübingen, 1910, pp. 115–118). The vast
literature of Rabbinic angelology and
demonology shows the same features—upon
which Conybeare (in *The Jewish Quarterly
Review*, xi. 1–45) has thrown considerable
light in his translation of *The Testament
of Solomon.*

It is a moot point as to whether these
Ḥasidim are the lineal descendants of the
saintly party known by that name in the
Maccabean epoch. The point, however,
which clearly emerges is, that a certain
esoteric wisdom and capacity for doing
things, unknown to the multitudes, was
vouchsafed to certain bodies of men, who by
the superior purity of their living, by their
unabated devotion to the things of the spirit,
and by their cultivation of a kind of brotherhood in which simplicity, single-mindedness,
and charity were the reigning virtues, were
enabled to enjoy a living in the world of the
unseen.

One further matter, in conclusion. The
interests of historical accuracy demand that,
as has been already pointed out, the student
should be in no hurry to say that these
esoteric sects whose beliefs are so vaguely

and fragmentarily described in the Rabbinic
literature, are to be identified with the
Essenes described in the writings of Philo
and Josephus. Resemblances there certainly are, but there are differences too ;
and the Rabbinic allusions are too disjointed
to enable one to form an impression—even
an inexact impression, leave alone an exact
one—of the lives and thoughts of these
mystic gatherings. Philo and Josephus
paint a complete picture. The Talmud and
Midrashim give but stray and elusive hints.
For one thing, the Essenes practised celibacy ;
marriage must necessarily dissolve the fellowship characterising the order. The Rabbinic
records give no hint of the duty of celibacy.
On the contrary, marriage was held to pro-
mote a far higher sanctity than celibacy.
But the Rabbis tolerated some exceptional
cases of celibacy ; so that it is difficult
to speak categorically. Again, the centre of
gravity of Essenic religion seems to have
been the cultivation of the highest ethics.
They stressed *inward* religion as demanded
by the Mosaic code, but, with the exception
of a reverence for the holiness of the Sabbath,
they were comparatively unconcerned with
the *outward* religious duties incumbent upon
the Jews of that time. Thus, they made
little or nothing of the sacrifices—doubtless
a corollary of their emphasis on the allegorical interpretation of Scripture. But it

was otherwise with the early mystics of the
Rabbinic literature. Although living in an
atmosphere of mystery and looking to the
Divine secret to unroll itself at any moment,
they yet never overlooked the claims of
institutional religion; they never flouted
the ceremonial side of Judaism; they were
inflexible upholders of the Law and its
associated traditions. The same phenomenon is, of course, seen in the history of
Christian mysticism where the first-hand,
inward, individualised experiences of the
ground-truths of religion are conformed to
the prevailing and accredited dogmas of
Christianity.

There were mystics among the Pharisees
as well as among the Essenes, and yet we
are told that the most spiritually-gifted
among the former (who constituted a
habūrah, *i.e.* ' fellowship ') were they who
were most scrupulous about the giving
of the priestly dues—a purely external
religious duty based on the legalism of the
Pentateuch. Indeed this blending of
legalism with spirituality, this consistent
(and successful) interweaving of the formalism of tradition with the mysticism of the
individual, is an arresting feature of Jewish
theology in all ages.

In fine, as must be apparent from the
general trend and contents of this book,
the whole of Jewish mysticism is really

nothing but a commentary on the Jewish
Bible, an attempt to pierce through to its
most intimate and truest meaning; and
what is the Bible to the Jew but the ad-
monisher to be loyal to the traditions of
his fathers? Only then will he find God
when he is convinced that He was found of
those of his race who sought Him in an
earlier day.

CHAPTER II

THE MERKABAH (CHARIOT) MYSTICISM

THE first chapter of Ezekiel has played a most fruitful part in the mystical speculations of the Jews. The lore of the heavenly Throne-chariot in some one or other of its multitudinous implications is everywhere to be met with. Whence Ezekiel derived these baffling conceptions of the Deity, and what historical or theological truths he meant to portray by means of them, are themes with which the scholars of the Old Testament have ever busied themselves. But the Jewish mystic sought no rationalistic explanation of them. He took them as they were, in all their mystery, in all their strange and inexplicable fantasy, in all their weird aloofness from the things and ideas of the everyday life. He sought no explanation of them because he was assured that they stood for something which did not need explaining. He *felt* instinctively that the Merkabah typified the human longing for the sight of the Divine Presence and companionship with it. To attain this end was, to him, the acme of all spiritual life.

Ezekiel's image of Yahve riding upon the chariot of the ' living creatures,' accompanied by sights and voices, movements and upheavals in earth and heaven, lying outside the range of the deepest ecstatic experiences of all other Old Testament personages, was for the Jewish mystic a real opening, an unveiling, of the innermost and impenetrable secrets locked up in the inter-relation of the human and the divine. It was interpreted as a sort of Divine self-opening, self-condescension to man. The door is flung wide open so that man, at the direct invitation of God, can come to the secret for which he longs and seeks. This idea is a supreme factor in the mystic life of all religions. The soul is urged on to seek union with God, only because it feels that God has first gone out, on His own initiative and uninvited, to seek union with it. The human movement from within is but a response to a larger Divine movement from without. The call has come; the answer must come.

The Chariot (Merkabah) was thus a kind of ' mystic way ' leading up to the final goal of the soul. Or, more precisely, it was the mystic ' instrument,' the vehicle by which one was carried direct into the ' halls ' of the unseen. It was the aim of the mystic to be a 'Merkabah-rider,' so that he might be enabled, while still in the trammels of the flesh, to mount up to his spiritual Eldorado. Whether, as has been suggested, the uncanny imagery of the Merkabah lore is to be sought, for its origin, in the teachings of Mithraism, or, as has also been suggested, in certain branches of Mohammedan mysticism, one can see quite clearly how its governing idea is based on a conception general to all the mystics, *viz.* that the quest for the ultimate Reality is a kind of pilgrimage, and the seeker is a traveller towards his home in God.

It was remarked, on a previous page, that the mystic neither asked, nor waited, for any rationalistic explanation of the Merkabah mysteries. He felt that they summarised for him the highest pinnacle of being towards the realisation of which he must bend his energies without stint. But yet, from certain stray and scattered Rabbinic remarks, one takes leave to infer that there existed in the early Christian centuries a small sect of Jewish mystics—the elect of the elect—to whom certain measures of instruction were given in these recondite themes. There was an esoteric science of the Merkabah. What its content was we can only dimly guess—from the Rabbinic sources. It appears to have been a confused angelology, one famous angel Metatron playing a conspicuous part.

Much more is to be found in the early Enoch-
literature as well as—from quite other points
of view—in the mediæval Kabbalah.   Let us
give some illustrative sayings from the
Rabbinic literature.

In the Mishna, Ḥaggigah, ii. 1, it is said :
" It is forbidden to explain the first chapters
of Genesis to *two* persons, but it is only to be
explained to *one* by himself.   It is forbidden
to explain the Merkabah even to *one* by himself unless he be a sage and of an original
turn of mind."   In a passage in *T.B.*
Ḥaggigah, 13a, the words are added : " but it
is permitted to divulge to him [*i.e.* to *one* in
the case of the first chapters of Genesis] the
first words of the chapters."   In the same
passage another Rabbi (Zeʻera) of the 3rd
century A.D. remarks, with a greater strin-
gency : " We may not divulge even the first
words of the chapters [neither of Genesis nor
Ezekiel] unless it be to a ' chief of the Beth
Din ' [1] or to one whose heart is tempered by
age or responsibility."

Yet another teacher of the same century
declares in the same connection : " We may
not divulge the secrets of the Torah to any
but to him to whom the verse in *Isaiah*, iii. 3,
applies, *viz.* the captain of fifty and the
honourable man, and the counsellor and the
cunning artificer and the eloquent orator."

---

[1] Literally ' House of Judgment,' the technical name for
a Jewish Court of Law.

(The Rabbis understood these terms to mean distinction in a knowledge and practice of the Torah.)

This insistence upon a high level of moral and religious fitness as the indispensable prelude to a knowledge of the Merkabah has its counterpart in the mysticism of all religions. The organic life, the self, conscious and unconscious, must be moulded and developed in certain ways ; there must be an education, moral, physical, emotional ; a psychological adjustment, by stages, of the mental states which go to the make-up of the full mystic consciousness. As Evelyn Underhill (*Mysticism*, p. 107) says : " Mysticism shows itself not merely as an attitude of mind and heart, but as a form of organic life. . . . It is a remaking of the whole character on high levels in the interests of the transcendental life."

That the Rabbis were fully alive to the importance of this self-discipline is seen by a remark of theirs in *T.B. Ḥaggigah*, 13a, as follows : " A certain youth was once explaining the Ḥashmal (*Ezekiel*, i. 27, translated ' amber ' in the A.V.) when fire came forth and consumed him." When the question is asked, Why was this ? the answer is : " His time had not yet come " (*lāv māti zimnēh*). This cannot but mean that his youthful age had not given him the opportunities for the mature self-culture necessary to the mystic apprehension. The Ḥashmal, by the way, was interpreted by the Rabbis as : (a) a shortened form of the full phrase *ḥāyot ĕsh mē-māl-lē-loth*, *i.e.* 'the living creatures of fire, speaking'; or (b) a shortened form of *'ittim ḥāshoth ve-'ittim mĕ-mǎl-lĕ-lōth*, *i.e.* 'they who at times were silent and at times speaking.' In the literature of the mediæval Kabbalah, the Ḥashmal belongs to the 'Yetsiratic' world (*i.e.* the abode of the angels, presided over by Metatron who was changed into fire; and the spirits of men are there too).[1] According to a modern Bible commentator (the celebrated Russian Hebraist, M. L. Malbim, 1809–1879) the word signifies "the Ḥayot [*i.e.* 'living creatures' of *Ezekiel*, i.] which are the abode [or camp] of the Shechinah [*i.e.* Divine Presence] where there is the 'still small voice.' It is they [*i.e.* the Ḥayot] who receive the Divine effluence from above and disseminate it to the Ḥayot who are the movers of the 'wheels' [of Ezekiel's Chariot]."

Many more passages of a like kind might be quoted in support of the view that the attainment of a knowledge of the Merkabah was a hard quest beset with ever so many impediments; that it pre-supposed, on the one hand, an exceptional measure of self-development, and, on the other, an extra-

---

[1] There were four such 'worlds' in the mediæval Kabbalah. They will be alluded to further on.

ordinary amount of self-repression and self-renouncement.

But the mention of *fire* in the preceding paragraph leads us to the consideration of an aspect of the Merkabah which brings the latter very much into line with the description of mystical phenomena in literature generally. Every one knows how the image of fire dominates so much of the mysticism of Dante. The mediæval Christian mystics —Ruysbroeck, Catherine of Genoa, Jacob Boehme, and others—appeal constantly to the same figure for the expression of their deepest thoughts on the relations between man and the Godhead. The choice of the metaphor probably rests on the fact that ' fire ' can be adapted to symbolise either or both of the following truths : (*a*) the brightness, illumination which comes when the goal has been reached, when the quest for the ultimate reality has at last been satisfied ; (*b*) the all-penetrating, all-encompassing, self-diffusing force of fire is such a telling picture of the mystic union of the soul and God. The two are inter-penetrated, fused into one state of being. The soul is red-hot with God, who at the same time, like fire, holds the soul in his grip, dwells in it.

Examples are the following: In the *Midrash Rabba* on *Canticles*, i. 12, it is said : " Ben 'Azzai [a famous Rabbi of the 2nd century A.D.] was once sitting expounding the

Torah. *Fire surrounded him.* They went
and told R. 'Akiba, saying, ' Oh ! Rabbi !
Ben 'Azzai is sitting expounding the Torah,
and *fire is lighting him up on all sides.*'
Upon this, R. 'Akiba went to Ben 'Azzai and
said unto him, ' I hear that thou wert sitting
expounding the Torah, with the *fire playing
round about thee.*' ' Yes, that is so,' replied
he. ' Wert thou then,' retorted 'Akiba,
' engaged in unravelling the secret chambers
of the Merkabah ? ' ' No,' replied he." It
is not germane here to go into what the sage
said he really was engaged in doing. The
quotation sufficiently shows how in the 2nd
century A.D. the imagery of fire was tradition-
ally associated with esoteric culture.

Here is another instance, in *T.B. Succah,*
28a. Hillel the Elder (30 B.C.–10 A.D.) had
eighty disciples. Thirty of them were
worthy enough for the Shechinah to rest
upon them. Thirty of them were worthy
enough for the sun to stand still at their
bidding. The other twenty were of average
character. The greatest among them all
was Jonathan son of Uziel (1st century A.D.) ;
the smallest among them all was Johanan
son of Zaccai (end of 1st century A.D.).
The latter, smallest though he was, was
acquainted with every conceivable branch
of both exoteric and esoteric lore. He knew
' the talk of the ministering angels and the
talk of the demons and the talk of the palm-

trees (*děkālim*).' He knew also the lore of the Merkabah. Such being the measure of the knowledge possessed by ' the smallest,' how great must have been the measure of the knowledge possessed by 'the greatest,' *viz.* Jonathan son of Uziel! When the latter was sitting and studying the Torah (presumably the esoteric lore of the angels and the Merkabah) every bird that flew above him was burnt by fire. These latter words are the description of the ecstatic state, the moments of exaltation, the indescribable peace and splendour which the soul of the mystic experiences when, disentangling itself from the darkness of illusion, it reaches the Light of Reality, the condition so aptly phrased by the Psalmist who said: "For with thee is the fountain of life; in thy light shall we see light " (*Psalm,* xxxvi. 9). The bird flying in the environment of this unrestrained light, must inevitably be consumed by the fire of it.

The monument which Jonathan son of Uziel has left us in perpetuation of his mystical tendencies, is his usage of the term Memra (' Word ') to denote certain phases of Divine activity, in the Aramaic Paraphrase to the Prophets which ancient Jewish tradition assigned to his authorship, but which modern research has shown to be but the foundation on which the extant Aramaic Paraphrase to the Prophets rests.

Another illustration of the mystic vision of light consequent on the rapture created by an initiation into the Merkabah mysteries is related in *T.B. Ḥaggigah*, 14b, as follows :

" R. Joḥanan son of Zaccai was once riding on an ass, and R. Eliezer son of Arach was on an ass behind him. The latter Rabbi said to the former, 'O master! teach me a chapter of the Merkabah mysteries.' 'No!' replied the master, 'Have I not already informed thee that the Merkabah may not be taught to any one man by himself unless he be a sage and of an original turn of mind ?' 'Very well, then!' replied Eliezer son of Arach. 'Wilt thou give me leave to tell thee a thing which thou hast taught me ?' 'Yes!' replied Joḥanan son of Zaccai. 'Say it!' Forthwith the master dismounted from his ass, wrapped himself up in a garment, and sat upon a stone beneath an olive tree. 'Why, O master, hast thou dismounted from thy ass ?' asked the disciple. 'Is it possible,' replied he, 'that I will ride upon my ass at the moment when thou art expounding the mysteries of the Merkabah, and the Shechinah is with us, and the ministering angels are accompanying us ?' Forthwith R. Eliezer son of Arach opened his discourse on the mysteries of the Merkabah, and no sooner had he begun, *than fire came down from heaven* and encompassed all the trees of the field, which, with one accord, burst into song. What song ? It was ' Praise the Lord from the earth, ye dragons and all deeps ; fruitful trees and all cedars, praise ye the Lord ' (*Psalm*, cxlviii. 7, 9). Upon this, an angel cried out from the fire, saying, ' Truly these, even these, are the secrets of the Merkabah.' R. Johanan son of Zaccai then arose and kissed his disciple upon the forehead, saying, ' Blessed be the Lord, God of Israel, who hath given unto Abraham our father a son who is able to understand, and search, and discourse upon, the mysteries of the Merkabah.' . . .

" When these things were told to R. Joshua [another disciple of Johanan], the latter said one day when walking with R. José the Priest [another disciple of Johanan], ' Let us likewise discourse about the Merkabah ! ' R. Joshua opened the discourse. It was a day in the height of summer. The heavens became a knot of thick clouds, and something like a rainbow was seen in the clouds, and the ministering angels came in companies to listen as men do to hear wedding music. R. José the Priest went and told his master of it, who exclaimed, ' Happy are ye, happy is she that bare you ! Blessed are thy eyes that beheld these things ! Indeed I saw myself with you in a dream, seated upon Mount Sinai, and I heard a

heavenly voice exclaiming, Ascend hither!
Ascend hither! large banqueting-halls and
fine couches are in readiness for you. You
and your disciples, and your disciples'
disciples, are destined to be in the third set'
[*i.e.* the third of the three classes of angels
who, as the Rabbis taught, stand continually before the Shechinah, singing psalms
and anthems]."

There are several points which need
making clear in this remarkable passage.
The objection to discuss the Merkabah while
sitting on the animal's back, and the fact
of sitting upon a stone under an olive tree,
point to the necessary physical and tempera-
mental self-discipline which is the *sine quâ
non* of the mystic's equipment in all ages
and among all nations. He must not be
set high on the ass, lest his heart be lifted up
too. He must be cleansed of every vestige
of pride, lowly and of contrite spirit. It
has been mentioned in the previous chapter
how meekness was one of the unfailing
qualities of the *Zen'uim*. The proud man,
said the Rabbis, "crowds out the feet of the
Shechinah." "Whosoever is haughty will
finally fall into Gehinnom." Pride, to the
Rabbis, was the most terrible pitfall in the
path of the religious life. Its opposite,
humility, was the starting-point of all the
virtues. If such was the premium placed
upon meekness in so far as it concerned the

life of the ordinary Jew, how enormous
must have been its importance for the life
of the mystic—for him who aimed at knowing
Eternal Truth ? Everything that savours
of evil, of imperfection, of sin, must vanish.
The primary means of this self-purification
is the culture of humility.

The remark that 'the Shechinah is with
us and the ministering angels are accompanying us' emphasises two salient features of Rabbinic mysticism. Firstly, the
Shechinah is the transcendent-immanent God
of Israel ; Israel's environment was saturated with the Shechinah whose unfailing
companionship the Jew enjoyed in all the
lands of his dispersion. "Even at the time
when they are unclean does the Shechinah
dwell with them," runs a passage in *T.B.*
Yoma, 57a. How unique, how surpassingly
vivid must have been the consciousness
of this accompanying Shechinah-Presence
to the Merkabah initiates, to those who had
raised themselves so high above the level
of the ordinary crowd by the pursuit of an
ideal standard of self-perfection ! Secondly,
the 'ministering angels' play a large part
in all the Merkabah lore, as is seen from the
following Rabbinic comments.

Ezekiel, i. 15, says, "Now as I beheld the
living creatures, behold one wheel upon the
earth by the living creatures, with his four
faces." R. Eliezer said, "There is one angel

who stands upon earth but whose head reaches
to the ' living creatures ' . . . his name is
Sandalphon. He is higher than his neighbour [1] to the extent of a five-hundred years'
journey. He stands behind the Merkabah
wreathing coronets for his Master " (*T.B.
Ḥaggigah*, 13b).

Another passage reads : " Day by day
ministering angels are created from the stream
of fire. They sing a pæan [to God] and then
pass away, as it is said, ' They are new every
morning ; great is thy faithfulness ' (*Lamentations*, iii. 23). . . . From each word that
comes forth from the mouth of the Holy
One (blessed be He) there is created one angel,
as it is said, ' By the word of the Lord were
the heavens made and all the host of them by
the breath of his mouth ' " (*Psalm*, xxxiii. 6).

The Rabbis obviously understood the
phrase ' the host of them ' to refer, not as we
suppose, to the paraphernalia of the heavens,
i.e. the stars, planets, etc., but to the angelic
worlds. The idea of the Word of God becoming transformed into an angel, and hence
accomplishing certain tangible tasks among
men, here on earth, bears strong resemblances
to the Logos of Philo as well as to the
Prologue of the Fourth Gospel.

The phrase to ' listen as men do to hear
wedding music ' (or literally ' the music of
bride and bridegroom ') is a reminiscence of

----

[1] Sandalphon = Greek συνάδελφος = co-brother.

the large mass of Rabbinic mysticism clustering round the love overtures of bride and
bridegroom in the Book of Canticles. The
book, on the Rabbinic interpretation, teaches
the great truth of a ' spiritual marriage '
between the human and the Divine, a be-
trothal between God and Israel. " In ten
places in the Old Testament," says *Canticles
Rabba*, iv. 10, " are the Israelites designated as
a ' bride,' six here [*i.e.* in the Book of Can-
ticles] and four in the Prophets . . . and in
ten corresponding passages is God represented
as arrayed in garments [which display the
dignity of manhood in the ideal bridegroom]."

To the minds of the Rabbis, the super-
abundant imagery of human love and marriage
which distinguishes Canticles from all other
books of the Old Testament, was the truest
symbol of the way in which human Israel and
his Divine Father were drawn near to one
another. The intimate and secret experiences of the soul of the Jew, the raptures of
its intercourse with God in senses which no
outsider could understand, were best re-
flected in the language of that august and
indefinable passion which men call love.

The remark ' ascend hither ! ascend hither !
large banqueting halls and fine couches are
in readiness for you,' etc., points to another
prominent phase of Rabbinic mysticism. It
was strongly believed that the pious could,
by means of a life led on the highest plane,

free themselves from the trammels that bind
the soul to the body and enter, living, into
the heavenly paradise. The idea was obviously a development of a branch of Old
Testament theology. But the latter gets no
further than the conception that heaven may
be reached without dying, the persons translated thither having finished their earthly
career. The experiences of Enoch (*Genesis,*
v. 24) and of Elijah (2 *Kings,* ii. 11) are illustrations. A development of the doctrine is
the thought that certain favoured saints of
history are, after death and when in heaven,
given instruction concerning the doings of
men and the general course of events here
below. The Apocalyptic literature (see
especially *Apocalypse of Baruch,* by Dr.
Charles) deals somewhat largely in this idea ;
and there are traces of it in the Rabbinical
literature. But these saints, however true
the teachings and revelations vouchsafed to
them may eventually have turned out to be,
are *dead* as far as the world is concerned.

A further development is seen in the theory
that certain pious men may temporarily
ascend into the unseen, and, having seen and
learnt the deepest mysteries, may return to
earth again. These were the mystics who,
by training themselves to a life of untarnished
holiness, were able to fit themselves for
entering a state of ecstasy, to behold visions
and hear voices which brought them into

direct contact with the Divine Life. They were the students of the Merkabah who, as a result of their peculiar physical and mental make-up, were capable of reaching the goal of their quest. " There were four men," says the Talmud (*Haggigah*, 14b), " who entered Paradise." They were R. 'Akiba (50–130 A.D.), Ben 'Azzai (2nd century A.D.), Ben Zoma (2nd century A.D.), and Elisha b. Abuyah (end of 1st century and beginning of 2nd century A.D.). Although this passage is one of the puzzles of the Talmud, and is variously interpreted, we may quite feasibly lay it down that the reference here is to one of those waking visits to the invisible world which fall within the experiences of all mystics in all ages.

Fragments of what was a large mystic literature of the later Rabbinical epoch (*i.e.* from about the 7th to the 11th century, usually known as the Gaonic epoch) have descended to us. Of these, one branch is the *Hekalot* (*i.e.* ' halls '), which are supposed to have originated with the mystics of the fore-mentioned period who called themselves *Yōrĕdē Merkabah* (*i.e.* Riders in the Chariot). As Dr. Louis Ginzberg says (see art ' Ascension ' in *Jewish Encyc.* vol. ii.), " these mystics were able, by various manipulations, to enter into a state of autohypnosis, in which they declared they saw heaven open before them, and beheld its mysteries. It was believed that he only could undertake this

Merkabah-ride, who was in possession of all
religious knowledge, observed all the com-
mandments and precepts and was almost
superhuman in the purity of his life. This,
however, was regarded usually as a matter of
theory ; and less perfect men also attempted,
by fasting and prayer, to free their senses
from the impressions of the outer world and
succeeded in entering into a state of ecstasy
in which they recounted their heavenly
visions."

Much of this belief survives in modern
Jewish mysticism, whose chief representatives
known as Hasidim are to be found in Russia,
Poland, Galicia, and Hungary.

Although it was stated above that the
large volume of this phase of mystic literature originated in the period from the 7th
to the 11th century, modern research has
clearly proved that its roots go back to a
very much earlier date. In fact, it is very
doubtful whether its origin is to be looked for
at all in the bosom of early Judaism. Mithra-
worship is now taken by scholars to account
for much of it. But it is hazardous to ven-
ture any final opinion. It must never be
forgotten that the first chapter of Ezekiel
worked wonders on the old Hebrew imagination. Commentaries on almost every
word in the chapter were composed whole-
sale. In all likelihood, the mysticism of the
Merkabah-riders is a syncretism. Mithraic

conceptions in vogue were foisted on to
the original Jewish interpretations ; and, in
combination with Neo-Platonism, there was
evolved this branch of Jewish mysticism which,
though by no means abundant in the Talmud
and the Midrashim, occupies a considerable
place in the ideas of the mediæval Kabbalah,
as well as in the tenets of the modern
Ḥasidim.

CHAPTER III

PHILO : METATRON : WISDOM

SOMETHING must now be said about the mystical elements in the Hellenistic, as distinguished from the Palestinian, branch of early Judaism. The Palestinian (which includes the Babylonian) is, by a long way, the more voluminous; and its significance for the development of the later Judaism totally eclipses that of Jewish Hellenism which really wielded its influence over Christianity rather than over Judaism. Still there are a few outstanding features in Jewish Hellenism which are germane to our subject. Moreover, modern research has shown that there was a certain degree of intercourse, in the opening centuries of the Christian era, between Jewish scholars of Palestine and Babylonia on the one hand, and Jewish scholars of Alexandria on the other, Alexandria being the great centre of the Hellenistic culture then predominant. This must have resulted in an interchange and interaction of ideas and doctrines which found their way into the literatures of both branches.

A noteworthy example of this fusion of
ideas is the famous Philo Judæus of Alexandria. Platonic, Stoic and Rabbinic strata
make up the philosophy of Philo. They
are intermingled not always harmoniously.
But what tells hard upon the student of
Philo's presentation of Hebrew thought is
the difficulty of knowing whether certain
parallel ideas in his writings and the writings
of the Palestinian Rabbis originated with
him or with the Rabbis. It has, however,
been shown, with a fair approach to con-
clusiveness, that where there is a resemblance
in *Halachic* interpretation, Philo is the
borrower ; whereas the *Haggadic* parallels
emanate from the Rabbis.

To attempt an examination of Philo's
mysticism as a whole lies quite outside the
scope of this book. All that can be dealt
with—and this very fragmentarily and in-
adequately — are certain points in the
mysticism of his Logos idea which, by
reason of their affinity with the Haggadah,
are important to an understanding of Jewish
mysticism. How to bridge the chasm between God and the world, how at the first
creation of man it was possible for God
who is the all-holy and all-perfect, to come
into contact with imperfect man, is an oft-
recurring subject of speculation in the
Talmud and Midrashim. The cosmogony
of Genesis comes in for an exceptionally

elaborate treatment. In this connection
it is only to be expected that angelology
should figure largely. Theologians are quite
wrong when they say that post-Biblical
Judaism removed the Deity further and
further away from the world, and then
tried to bring Him nearer again by the
medium of the angel. The truth is that God
was in many senses brought very near, and
the angel was but an aspect of this ' nearness.' God was immanent as well as transcendent, and the angel was a sort of emanation of the Divine, an off-shoot of Deity,
holding intimate converse with the affairs
of the world. It was on these lines that the
Rabbis solved their problem of reconciling
the idea of a pure God with an impure
world. God did not really come into contact with the world, but His angels did—
and His angels are really part and parcel
of His own being, emanations of His own
substance. This was, of course, far from
being a logical solution, but the Rabbis,
like many other religious thinkers of those
early centuries, were not masters of logic.

Philo's ideas run in what seems a similar
groove. All matter is to him evil; hence
God must be placed outside the world. But
though this was his philosophy, his religion—
Judaism—taught him otherwise. Obliged
to find some way out of the difficulty, he
hit upon the idea of the Logoi, *i.e.* divine

agencies, which, while being in some senses inherent in God, are, in other ways and at various times, exterior to Him. It would be incorrect to say that he derived this theology from the Rabbinic sources. Platonic and Stoic teachings are largely responsible for them. But Philo endeavoured to bring them into line with Rabbinic modes of Biblical interpretation. He felt that he ought to give them a Jewish dress— with the result that much of what he says about Divine powers, agencies, attributes operating in the world, independently of the Deity and yet as part and parcel of Him, bears a close resemblance to much of Rabbinic angelology and Rabbinic teaching about the Divine attributes. Thus, to give some examples.

The Rabbis (in *Genesis Rabba*, viii. 3, 4, and in many other places) are at pains to justify the usage of the grammatical plural in the words : " And God said, Let us make man " (*Gen.* i. 26). Various opinions are thrown out. But the finally accepted view is that " at the time when God was about to create the first man, He took counsel with the ministering angels." What this interpretation aims at, is to relieve the Deity of the blame for the evil in man, and to place it upon some other shoulders. But what it really does is to show that the earth is the scene and centre of Divine agencies.

Angels are emanations of the Divine working here below. Man is in a *double* sense *made* by them. It was they who had a hand in his creation. It is they who fill his environment, and make him realise that he is ever in the grip of a Presence from which there is no escaping. The Talmud and Midrashim overflow with the descriptions of vast hierarchies of spiritual intelligences—angels— who guide the will of man and the course of nature, surrounding man on all sides and at all moments, shielding him and lifting him up to higher planes of thought and feeling. They protect the pious and help them in their transactions. Every angelic host consists of a thousand times a thousand. The angels give instruction in certain matters. Every man has a special guardian angel. All this literature of angelology can have no possible meaning at all unless it is interpreted to mean that God is present and active in the world, a Power behind phenomena, a directing Mind, a controlling Will, an Immanent God.

Philo's doctrine is similar. Thus he says : " For God, not condescending to come down to the external senses, sends His own words (*logoi*) or angels for the sake of giving assistance to those who love virtue. But they attend like physicians to the diseases of the soul, and apply themselves to heal them, offering sacred recommendations like sacred

laws, and inviting men to practise the duties
inculcated by them, and, like the trainers of
wrestlers, implanting in their pupils strength
and power and irresistible vigour. Very
properly, therefore, when he [*i.e.* Jacob] has
arrived at the external sense, he is represented no longer as meeting God, but only
the Divine word, just as his grandfather
Abraham, the model of wisdom did " (*On
Dreams*, i. 12).

In another passage in the fore-mentioned
section, he speaks of " the immortal words
(*logoi*) which it is customary to call angels "
(*ibid.* i. 19).   Again, take the following :

" But these men pray to be nourished by
the word (*logos*) of God. But Jacob, raising
his head above the word, says that he is
nourished by God Himself, and his words are
as follows : The God in whom my father
Abraham and Isaac were well pleased ; the
God who has nourished me from my youth
upwards to this day ; the angel who has
delivered me from all my evils, bless these
children. This now, being a symbol of a
perfect disposition, thinks God Himself his
nourisher, and not the word ; and he speaks
of the angel, which is the word, as the phy-
sician of his evils, in this speaking most
naturally. For the good things which he has
previously mentioned are pleasing to him,
inasmuch as the living and true God has
given them to him face to face, but the

secondary good things have been given to him
by the angels and by the word of God.   On
this account I think it is that God gives men
pure good health which is not preceded by
any disease in the body, by Himself alone,
but that health which is an escape from
disease, He gives through the medium of skill
and medical science, attributing it to science,
and to him who can apply it skilfully, though
in truth it is God Himself who heals both by
these means, and without these means.   And
the same is the case with regard to the soul.
The good things, namely, food, He gives to
men by His power alone ; but those which
contain in them a deliverance from evil, he
gives by means of His angels and His word "
(*Allegories of the Sacred Laws,* iii. 62).

The intermingling of Greek and Hebraic
elements in these passages is curious.   But
the two sets are easily distinguishable.   Two
things are clear from these quotations.
Firstly, the angel is a kind of representative of
the Deity among mortals.   It is a sort of
God in action.   God is very near man and
not transcendent.   Secondly, the angel and
the Logos (Word) or Logoi (Words) have
very much the same nature and fulfil very
much the same function.   The Rabbinic
mysticism clustering round angels as well as
the Rabbinic doctrine of the Shechinah—
which will be dealt with later—have likewise
many points in common.   Angels encompass

the worthy Israelite ; the Shechinah likewise accompanies Israel, nay, even dwells in the midst of impure Israelites, as a famous passage in the Talmud says.   But there are aspects of Philo's angelology which are strange to Rabbinic modes of thought.   One of the most interesting of these is his designation of angels as ' incorporeal intelligences ' and as ' immortal souls ' (*On Dreams,* i. 20). The Rabbis obviously thought of angels as material beings.   They even at times materialised the Shechinah, as will be mentioned in the following chapter.   The sight of an angel was a physical phenomenon. Philo's exegesis took quite a different turn.

Thus, in a lengthy comment on *Genesis,* xxviii. 12 (" And he dreamed a dream and behold a ladder was planted firmly on the ground, the head of which reached to heaven, and the angels of God were ascending and descending upon it ") he goes on to say : " This air is the abode of incorporeal souls, since it seemed good to the Creator of the universe to fill all parts of the world with living creatures. . . . For the Creator of the universe formed the air so that it should be the habit of those bodies which are immovable, and the nature of those which are moved in an invisible manner, and the soul of such as are able to exert an impetus and visible sense of their own. . . . Therefore, let no one deprive the most excellent nature of living creatures of the most excellent of those elements which surround the earth ; that is to say, of the air. For not only is it not alone deserted by all things besides, but rather like a populous city, it is full of imperishable and immortal citizens, souls equal in number to the stars. Now, of these souls some descend upon the earth with a view to being bound up in mortal bodies. . . . But some soar upwards. . . . But others, condemning the body of great folly and trifling, have pronounced it a prison and a grave, and, flying from it as from a house of correction or a tomb, have raised themselves aloft on light wings towards the æther, and have devoted their whole lives to sublime speculations. There are others again, the purest and most excellent of all, which have received greater and more divine intellects, never by any chance desiring any earthly thing whatever, but being, as it were, lieutenants of the Ruler of the universe, as though they were the eyes and ears of the great king, beholding and listening to everything. Now philosophers in general are wont to call these demons, but the sacred scriptures call them angels, using a name more in accord with nature. For indeed they do report (διαγγέλλουσι) the injunctions of the father to his children and the necessities of the children to the father " (*On Dreams*, i. 22).

From this passage the following deductions

seem to be obvious : Firstly, one large de-
partment of the Philonic angelology is utterly
strange to Talmudic and Midrashic exegesis.
An angel as an ' incorporeal soul ' is more akin
to the Aristotelian doctrine of 'intelligences,'
the intermediate beings between the Prime
Cause and existing things.   The general level
of the Rabbinic conception of the angel is
well characterised by the following passage:
    " When Samael saw that no sin was found
amongst them [the Jews] on the Day of
Atonement, he exclaimed before God, ' O
Thou Sovereign of the Universe, Thou hast
one nation on earth resembling the ministering angels in heaven. Just as the latter
are bare-footed, so are the Israelites bare-
footed on the Day of Atonement. Just as
the angels neither eat nor drink, so do the
Israelites not eat or drink on the Day of
Atonement. Just as the angels do not skip
about, so do the Israelites stand, unmoved,
upon their feet the whole Day of Atonement.
Just as peace reigns in the midst of the
angels, so does peace reign in the midst of
Israel on the Day of Atonement. Just as
the angels are free from all sin, so are the
Israelites free from sin on the Day of Atonement.' God hearkens to the advocacy of
Israel from the mouth of their arch-accuser,
and He grants His atonement for the altar,
for the sanctuary, and for the priests and for
all the people of the congregation."

This quotation is from the *Pirké-de-Rabbi-Eliezer*, a curious Midrashic work belonging to the 9th century A.D. It seems to summarise all the best points in the angelic lore of the Jews in the preceding nine centuries. The *naïveté* of the whole Rabbinic outlook is here very apparent and is ever so far removed from Philo's ' incorporeal soul.' In fact Philo's systematic division of angels into higher and lower grades is foreign to the Rabbinic speculations which are largely without any system whatsoever. Foreign also is his view of angels as ' souls descending upon the earth with a view to being bound up in mortal bodies.' The angel, in Rabbinic thought, is never *inside* any one.

But, in the second place, it is obvious to the student of *mediæval* as distinct from the *Talmudic* and *Midrashic* mysticism that there is an affinity between the Philonic treatment of angels and the treatment of the subject by such famous Jewish theologians as Sa'adia b. Joseph (892–942), Judah Ha-Levi (1085–1140), Solomon Ibn Gabirol (1021–1058), Abraham b. David (1100–1180), and Moses Maimonides (1135–1204). They, too, like Philo, were influenced by Greek thought—they were either Aristotelians, Platonists, or Neo-Platonists; so that what amount of influence came to them *directly* from the works of Philo is a matter that calls for deep research. To

the first-named theologian—Saʿadiah—there
is, like to Philo, something immaterial,
something ethereal, unearthly, about the
angel. While being *external* to man, it is,
in a sense, *internal* too, Saʿadiah being of
opinion that they were visions seen during
prophetic ecstasy rather than outward
realities. See his philosophical work
Emunot we-Deʿot ('Faith and Knowledge'),
ii. 8, iv. 6.

That Ibn Gabirol should develop a more
mystical line of thought than this, is
not surprising seeing he is dependent, in
many of his essential teachings, upon the
Enneads of Plotinus. The words of Judah
Ha-Levi are worth quoting here. He says
(*Cusari*, iv. 3):

" As for the angels, some are created for
the time being, out of the subtle elements of
matter [as air or fire]. Some are eternal
angels [*i.e.* existing from everlasting to
everlasting], and perhaps they are the
spiritual intelligences of which the philosophers speak. We must neither accept
nor reject their words [*i.e.* the words of these
philosophers]. It is doubtful whether the
angels seen by Isaiah, Ezekiel, and Daniel
were of the class of those created for the
time being or of the class of spiritual
essences which are eternal. ' The glory of
God ' is a thin subtle body (*goof dăk*) produced by the will of God, and which forms

itself in the prophet's imagination in the
way that the Divine will directs. This is
according to the first [*i.e.* simpler explana-
tion]. But according to a second [*i.e.* more
complex] explanation, the 'glory of God'
denotes the whole class of angels together
with the spiritual instruments (*kēlīm hā-
ruḥniim*), *viz.* the Throne, the Chariot
(*Merkabah*), the Firmament, the Ophanim
and the Spheres (*Gālgālīm*), and others
besides which belong to the things which
are eternal. All this is implied in the term
' glory of God.'

Further on, in the same paragraph, Judah
Ha-Levi brackets together as having one
meaning, the phrases 'Glory of God,' ' King-
dom of God,' and ' Shechinah of God.'
Maimonides speaks on the subject thus
(*Guide of the Perplexed*, ii. 6):

" The angels are not corporeal ; this is
what Aristotle also said ; only there is a
difference of name ; he calls them ' separate
intelligences ' (*sichlim nifrādīm*), whereas we
designate them angels. Moreover, when he
says that these ' separate intelligences ' are
also intermediaries between the Creator and
existing things, and that through their means
the spheres are moved—the motion of the
spheres being the prime cause of all being—
this also is written in all books, because you
will not find that God does any deed except
by means of an angel. . . . The movement of

Balaam's ass was done by means of an angel
. . . even the elements are called angels. . . .
The term angel is applied to a messenger of
men, as, *e.g.*, in the phrase 'and Jacob sent
messengers ' (*mălākīm*), in *Genesis*, xxxii. 3.
It is applied to a prophet, as, *e.g.*, in the
phrase ' and an angel of the Lord went up
from Gilgal to Bochim,' in *Judges*, ii. 1.
It is the term used of the ' separate intelligences ' which are seen by the prophets
in the prophetic vision. It is the designation also of the vital powers as we shall
explain."

Maimonides takes a Rabbinic apothegm
such as " God does nothing without previously consulting his heavenly [or upper]
host," or "God and his Court of Justice
have taken counsel together over every limb
in the human body, and have put each in its
rightful place," and is at pains to show how
these statements must not be taken literally
to mean that the Deity asks advice or seeks
help, but that what they convey is that the
term ' angel ' stands for the powers embodied
in all earthly phenomena, the world-forces
which are outflowings of God and represent
the aspect of the Divine activity in the
universe. Paradoxically enough, Maimonides
is rationalist and mystic at one and the same
time. While striving to strip the Hebrew
scriptures of the supernatural and the
miraculous, he exhibits his strong belief in a

world impregnated with traces and symp-
toms of a Divine Life.

But let it not be thought that Philo's
Logos and Logoi and his angelology are
nothing but symbols of abstract thinking
on the ways in which the Deity participates
in the affairs of men and of the world. It
has been mentioned a little above, that the
Rabbis often materialised the Shechinah
and gave strongly definite personality to
their ' angels.' There is one respect in which
Philo followed a similar line of exposition.
He too gave personality to his Logos—
personality as understood in Philo's time,
and very different from our modern ideas of
personality. Not alone does he speak of the
Logos as the being who guided the patriarchs,
as the angel who appeared to Hagar, as
the cloud at the Red Sea, as the Divine form
who changed the name of Jacob to Israel,
but he also describes him as " a suppliant
to the immortal God on behalf of the mortal
race which is exposed to affliction and
misery ; and is also the ambassador sent by
the Ruler of all to the subject race " (*Who
is Heir to the Divine Things*, xlii.). He is
" an attendant on the one Supreme Being "
(*ibid.* xlviii.). He is a paraclete. " For it
was indispensable that the man who was
consecrated to the Father of the world,
should have, as a paraclete, his son, the being
most perfect in virtue, to procure forgiveness

of sins, and a supply of unlimited blessings "
(*Life of Moses*, iii. 14).

The resemblances between these teachings
and much of the mysticism of Paul, as well
as of the author of the Fourth Gospel, are
unmistakable ; and whether they show
borrowing or are explicable as belonging to
the modes of thinking current in that age, is
a moot point. But what strongly concerns
our presentation of this subject, is the fact
that this branch of Philonic theology is
mirrored in the early Jewish, as well as in
the early Christian, teaching about God.
But with this considerable difference—that
whereas some of the cardinal doctrines of
Christianity are embedded in these ideas,
their significance for Judaism was, at no
epoch, vital. They belong to the *literature*,
not to the *faith*, of the Jew. They were
ever for the few rather than for the many.

It is to the figure of Metatron that we must
turn for the counterpart in Rabbinic mysticism to the personified Logos of Philo.
" Behold I send an angel before thee, to keep
thee in the way and to bring thee into the
place which I have prepared. Beware of
him and obey his voice, provoke him not ;
for he will not pardon your transgressions ;
for my name is in him " (*Exodus*, xxiii. 20, 21).
This angel in whom God's name exists is,
said the Rabbis, Metatron. And why so ?
Because, said they, the numerical value of

the Hebrew letters composing the name
Metatron (314) corresponds with those comprising the word Shaddai (= Almighty, one
of the Divine appellations).

This is a typical illustration of the Rabbinic
mysticism clustering round (i.) arithmetical
numbers, and (ii.) the Divine Name. ' My
name is in him,' *i.e.* the name ' Almighty '
is comprehended in the name ' Metatron.'
And the Divine Name is not merely a
grammatical part of speech. It is a kind of
essence of the Deity Himself. Hence, the
essence of the Deity exists in Metatron. He
is God's lieutenant. He represents the active
phase of Deity as manifested in the universe.

The command to ' beware of him and
obey his voice,' failing which ' he will not
pardon your transgressions,' forcibly brings
out the intercessory powers of Metatron. In
the Midrash *Tanḥuma* (on portion *Wa'-eth-
ḥanan*) it is graphically related how Moses,
when he knew that he must die, implored all
the different parts of creation—the sea, the
dry land, the mountains and the hills—to
pray that he might live. But they all
refuse. He finally betakes himself to
Metatron and says to him : " Seek mercy for
me that I may not die." But Metatron
replies : " O Moses, my master, why troublest
thou thyself thus ? I have heard behind the
veil that thy prayer for life will not be heard."
Metatron confesses that his intercession would

be vain, but yet—and here is a great point—
the Midrashic passage in question states that
immediately after " the anger of the Holy
Spirit grew cool."   Metatron did not succeed
in securing a prolongation of life for Moses,
but he managed to turn away Divine wrath
from him.

The title ' Prince of the Presence ' (*Sār
Hā-Pānim*) as well as ' Prince of the World '
(*Sar Ha-'Ōlam*) is often applied to Metatron.
A striking passage again depicting Metatron,
not alone as pleader for Israel, but as taking
upon himself the sorrow for Israel's sins, is
as follows (*Introduction to Lamentations
Rabba*, xxiv.) :

" No sooner was the Temple burnt than
the Holy One (blessed be He) said : Now will
I withdraw my Shechinah from it and I will
go up to my former habitation, as it is said
(*Hosea*, v. 15), ' I will go and return to my
place, till they acknowledge their offence and
seek my face.'   At that hour the Holy One
(blessed be He) wept, saying : Woe is me !
What have I done !   I caused my Shechinah
to abide below for the sake of Israel, but
now that Israel has sinned I have returned
to my original dwelling-place.   Far be it
from me that I should be a derision to the
nations and a mocking to all creatures !
Forthwith *Metatron fell upon his face*, exclaiming : O Sovereign of the Universe, let
me weep, but weep thou not ! "

The title ' Prince of the Presence ' or
' Prince of the World ' denotes Metatron's
active interference with the happenings of
the universe. *T.B. Yebamoth,* 16b, has the
following extraordinary saying :

" No one but the ' Prince of the World '
could have uttered verse 25 of *Psalm,* xxxvii,
' I have been young and now am old ; yet
have I not seen the righteous forsaken, nor
his seed begging bread.' Who else could
have said this ? Could God have said it ?
Does old age apply to God ? Could David
have said it ? Was he advanced in years
[when he composed this Psalm] ? No one
else but the ' Prince of the World ' could
have said it."

Two important ideas are enshrined here.
Firstly, Metatron's existence is made to date
from the Creation. A kind of pre-existence
is accorded him — and the doctrine of
pre-existence, or rather pre-existences, is a
ubiquitous element in the old Rabbinic
treatment of cosmogony. " Seven things
preceded the Creation of the world, *viz.* : (*a*)
the Torah, (*b*) the Divine Throne, (*c*) the
Temple, (*d*) the Name of the Messiah, (*e*)
Paradise, (*f*) Hell, (*g*) Repentance." Whether
Metatron ought to be an eighth, or is to be
identified with one among these seven, is a
point for further research.

Secondly, Metatron speaks words of worldly
wisdom garnered from an intimate ex-

perience of contact with the multitudinous facts and phases of earthly existence. He knows men as no one else could know them. He resembles, in this respect, the strongly-personified ' Wisdom ' of the Jewish-Alexandrian literature. Like it, he is given a sort of prime part in the cosmic process.

The Aramaic commentary (Targum) on *Genesis*, v. 24 ("And Enoch walked with God ; and he was not, for God took him ") renders the name ' Enoch ' by ' Metatron.' And just as Enoch in the Apocrypha (*Book of Jubilees*, iv. 23 ; 2 *Enoch*, liii. 2) appears as the heavenly scribe, so Metatron is often described in the Talmud and Midrash (see *T.B. Ḥaggigah*, 15a).

The idea fundamental to both these branches of literature is probably the same ; *viz.* that Metatron is a link uniting the human with the Divine, the bridge over which the knowledge of what is passing here below is brought to the realms above, and over which, in return, the Divine concern for men and the world passes down to the scenes of earth. A truly poetic rendering of this Divine concern is given in the Talmud (*Abodah Zarah*, 3b), where God is described as giving instruction a certain number of hours every day, to prematurely-deceased children. " Who instructed them in the period previous to their death ? " So the question runs. And the answer is " Meta-

tron ! " On this understanding, Metatron
is the helper to the Deity ; he, as it were,
takes up the Divine work at points where its
omnipotence cannot, if one may so speak,
reach ; not even the smallest, meanest
child need be forgotten, forsaken of God,
so long as Metatron is its guide and in-
structor.

Metatron has been identified with the
Zoroastrian Mithra. It certainly possesses
features resembling Philo's Logos. It has
also much in common with the theology of
the early Gnostics. In all probability it is
the result of a fusion of all these systems
of thought. The same can be predicted of
more than one other branch of Rabbinic
angelology. Noteworthy, however, is the
fact that though the Jews could get so far
as to bring themselves to look at Metatron
in the light of a heavenly co-worker with God,
a kind of semi-divinity having an access to
the Deity in a measure utterly unique, yet
so extraordinarily uncompromising were
their notions of the *Divine Unity* that, as
far as the religion of their daily life was
concerned, God alone was God, and Metatron
was ignored. His name figures somewhat
in certain departments of the Jewish liturgy.
He plays a *rôle* in mediæval Jewish
mysticism. But the stringent, inelastic
emphasis on the idea of safeguarding the
Divine Unity—an emphasis rarely appreci-

ated by the non-Jew—could brook no recognition of Metatron in the sphere of the
Jew's most intimate religious concerns.

One other dominating characteristic of
the Jewish-Hellenistic mysticism is to be
found in the functions assigned to the idea
of Wisdom. The grand preliminary to this
branch of doctrine is to be found in the Old
Testament (*Proverbs*, viii. 22–31) :

> The Lord possessed me in the beginning of his way,
>   before his works of old.
> I was set up from everlasting, from the beginning,
>   or ever the earth was.
> When there were no depths, I was brought forth ;
> When there were no fountains abounding with water.
> Before the mountains were settled, before the hills,
>   was I brought forth :
> While as yet he had not made the earth, nor the
>   fields, nor the highest part of the dust of the
>   world.
> When he prepared the heavens, I was there :
> When he set a compass upon the face of the depth :
> When he established the clouds above :
> When he strengthened the foundations of the deep :
> When he gave to the sea his decree
> That the waters should not pass his commandment :
> When he appointed the foundations of the earth :
> Then I was by him, as one brought up with him :
> And I was daily his delight,
> Rejoicing always before him ;
> Rejoicing in the habitable part of his earth,
> And my delights were with the sons of men.

Wisdom is the quality through which
God acts in the world, and by the instrumentality of which the Deity is known to

man. It is, in the passage just quoted,
personified and objectified. It dwells among
the sons of men and finds its special delight
in intercourse with them. It resembles the
Divine Pneuma or Spirit of the Stoic philosophy which, too, is given a prime part in
the cosmic process.

The Rabbis, it is interesting to notice,
made much of the phrase ' as one brought
up with him.' The phrase is represented
in the original Hebrew by one word ' *Amun.*'
By slight alterations in the vowelling they
extracted three meanings from it : *viz.*
(i.) pedagogue, (ii.) pupil, (iii.) workman.
Thus (i.) Wisdom (which they identified
with the Torah or Law) was the school-
master, tutor in the Divine household, giving
guidance to his Divine Master in his plans
for the creation of the universe. (ii.) Wisdom was the pupil or child of the Divine
(according to Rabbinic teaching a pupil
stood to his master in the position of child
to a father), hidden away by reason of its
preciousness in the lap of the Father, until
the time when it became a gift to a newly-
launched universe. (iii.) Wisdom was God's
workman, or servant, in the work and ad-
ministration of the universe.

And yet, in spite of all this obvious and
strong personification, Wisdom is but " a
quality belonging to God, one of His attributes by which He makes Himself known and

felt in the world of men and in the human
heart, one of the elements in the Divine
nature which is most in sympathy with the
innate tendency in man to go on striving
ever upward and onward." [1]

It is, after all, only God's Wisdom, no
matter how near an approach to personality
there may be in the various descriptions of
the term.   It is a potency wholly in God, and
yet at one and the same time wholly out of
God.   It is an embodiment, a revealer of one
aspect of Divine Spirit.   As has already been
remarked, the Jew always vindicated the *Unity
of God* no matter into what dubious fields his
theological speculations otherwise led him.

The apocryphal *Wisdom of Solomon* shows
forth   similar   mystical   elements.   " For
wisdom is more mobile than any motion ;
yea, she pervadeth and penetrateth all things
by reason of her pureness " (vii. 24).   This
is the Stoic conception of the immanent
Pneuma.   Again :

For she is a breath of the power of God,
And a clear effluence of the glory of the Almighty.

.   .   .   .

For she is an effulgence from everlasting light,
And an unspotted mirror of the working of God.

(vii. 25, 26.)

This seems to be rather the language of

[1] For a fuller treatment of this point see the author's
work, *The Immanence of God in Rabbinical Literature*,
pp. 198–201 (Macmillan & Co., 1912).

Platonism.   So is the following pronounce-
ment on the soul's pre-existence :

> For I was a witty child
> And had a good spirit,
> Yea, rather, being good, I came into a body unde-
>   filed.

(viii. 19, 20.)

Platonic, too, is the notion of earth and
matter pressing down the soul :

> For the corruptible body presseth down the soul,
> And the earthly tabernacle weigheth down
> The mind that museth upon many things.

(ix. 15.)

Wisdom is man's anchorage in time of
trouble.   It is the immanent protector and
redeemer of mankind.   The whole of chapter
x. is given over to this theme.   In xviii.
14–16, Wisdom becomes a personality.   It
is identified with the ' Word ' which dominates the Prologue of the Fourth Gospel, and
which in very similar senses appears in the
Rabbinic mysticism as ' Dibbur,' ' Mā-amār '
or ' Memra.'

> For while peaceful silence enwrapped all things,
> And night in her own swiftness was in mid-course,
> Thine all-powerful Word leaped from heaven out of
>   the Royal Throne,
> A stern warrior into the midst of the doomed land,
> Bearing as a sharp sword thine unfeigned command-
>   ment ;
> And standing, it filled all things with death ;
> And while it touched the heaven, it trode upon the
>   earth.

The Word in this extraordinary pronounce-
ment holds the idea of the Divine *Energy*
(as distinguished from the Divine *Love*)
which is operative in all things and which
" links the Transcendent Godhead with His
creative spirit, creature with Creator, and
man with man " (Evelyn Underhill, *The
Mystic Way*, p. 223). Truly enough, the
passage breathes what seems an unedifying
spirit of revenge and bloodthirstiness, but
it is explicable as an echo of the Old Testament idea of the God of righteousness who
hates wickedness and slays the wicked.
Divine Justice energises in the world, it is
embedded in the scheme of the cosmos,
it brooks no evil, it recognises nothing but
uprightness and truth. This idea of an
antagonism between an immanent God and
sin is, as will be seen in our next chapter,
a feature of the Rabbinic conception of
the Shechinah. In *Exodus Rabba*, xxviii. and
xxix., the Divine Voice at the revelation
on Sinai deals out death to the idolaters.
Similarly, the Targum (Aramaic paraphrase
on the Old Testament) renders the Hebrew
for " And my soul shall abhor you " (*Leviticus*, xxvi. 30), by " And my Memra [1] shall
remove you afar." The Memra here is the
avenger of the wayward Israelites. The

---

[1] ' Memra ' is the Aramaic for ' word.' For the full
theological significance of the ' Memra ' see the author's
Immanence of God in Rabbinical Literature, pp. 146–173.

Jewish-Hellenistic ' Wisdom,' the ' Word '
of the Fourth Gospel, the ' Memra ' of
Targumic literature, the ' Shechinah ' of
the Talmud and Midrashim—all point—
though in somewhat different ways and
degrees—to the great fact that the world
of matter and of spirit is the scene of the
immanent manifestation of Divine Wisdom,
Divine Power, Divine Love, Divine Justice.

CHAPTER IV

THE Old Testament, which alone is, and ever was, the Bible of the Jew, contains two oft-recurring ideas which rank among the principal elements of its theological teaching. These ideas are: (*a*) God as Father; (*b*) God as King. To give illustrations from the Old Testament is unnecessary, as the present work is not concerned with the theology of the Bible. It is our business to see in what ways they were developed by the Rabbis of the Talmud and Midrash, and adapted to their systems of thought about the relations between the Divine and the human. The fatherhood of God necessarily involves the sonship of man. The Rabbis living under the rule of foreign masters—the yoke of Rome and the memories of other yokes all equally galling—were loth to think that the oppressors of Israel could possibly enjoy so incomparably sublime a privilege as the Divine Fatherhood. It seemed a glaring contradiction that

nations who did not hold themselves bound
by the Mosaic code, should fall into the cate-
gory of ' sonship ' in relation to the Father.
Hence Fatherhood and Sonship became
limited to the Jew—although it should be
said, for the sake of historical accuracy,
that gleams of a far more comprehensive
outlook occasionally peep through the pages
of Rabbinic literature.

God's Fatherhood to the Jew is evidenced
by the outflow of His love towards him.
This love, which is ceaseless and rapturous,
is described by the Rabbis in numberless
ways—in parables, proverbs and similes
of a highly picturesque kind. The Jew is
possessed by the power of a Spirit of Love
which encircles him, holds him in its grip,
assures him that forgiveness, protection from
enemies, safety from mischief, every coveted
thing in heaven and earth, are his.

" Beloved are the Israelites," said R.
'Akiba (50–130 A.D.), " inasmuch as they
are called sons of God ; especially did that
love manifest itself in making known to
them that they are sons of God " (*Aboth*,
iii. 15). The same Rabbi declared the Book
of Canticles to be ' the holiest of all holy
books ' inasmuch as it symbolises the bond
of loving union in which Israel is joined to
God (*Canticles Rabba*, Introduction).

In a comment on *Deuteronomy*, xiv. i.
(" Ye are children unto the Lord your God ")

the *Sifri* states the conflicting opinions of two Rabbis. One of them asserts that the verse implies that the Israelites are only called children of God when they conduct themselves as children should, *i.e.* in the right way. The other maintains that the high privilege belongs to them even when they are wayward and sinful. The Father's love is with them no matter how little deserving they may be of it.

Strikingly poetical is the view given in the *Mechilta* (p. 30, Friedmann's ed.). Commenting on *Exodus*, xiv. 19 (" And the angel of the Lord which went before the camp of Israel, removed and went behind them "), it says : " Unto what may it be likened ? It may be likened unto a man who was walking by the way and leading his son before him. Robbers came to snatch the son away from him. Seeing this, the father removed the son from before him and placed him behind him. Then came a wolf behind him to steal the son away. So the father removed him from before him and placed him once again behind him. Then came the robbers from before him and the wolf from behind him in order to take the son away. What did the father do ? He took the son and placed him upon his arms. But the son thereupon began to feel the pain of the sun's heat upon him. So the father spread his mantle over him ; and when he felt hungry

he gave him food to eat, and when he felt
thirsty he gave him water. Likewise did
the Holy One (blessed be He) for Israel, as
it is said, ' And I taught Ephraim to go, I
took them on my arms ; but they knew not
that I healed them ' (*Hosea*, xi. 3). When
the son [Israel] felt the pain of the sun's heat,
He [the Father] spread his mantle over him,
as it is said, ' He spread a cloud for a covering ;
and fire to give light in the night ' (*Psalm*,
cv. 39). When he began to feel hunger, He
gave him food, as it is said, ' Behold, I will
rain bread from heaven for you ' (*Exodus*,
xvi. 4). When he began to feel thirst, He
gave him to drink, as it is said, ' And he
brought forth streams out of the rock '
(*Psalm*, lxxviii. 16)."

The truth enshrined in this parable—a
parable which has its counterparts in all
branches of the Rabbinic literature—is that
the closest and most loving of relationships
subsists between Israel and God. The love
of the Father forms an environment for
Israel. The atmosphere the latter breathes is
saturated with that love. His whole life is,
as it were, a response to it, infected with it,
absorbed in it. It gives him the sense of
a companionship with a greater and far
more real Life than himself. He is ever-
lastingly conscious of an intimate union
with a Power who can work all things for
him, because the governing motive of that

Power is Love.   Israel and the Father are one.

The Rabbis summarised all the far-reaching implications of this deeply mystical thought of Fatherhood by the usage of the term ' Shechinah.'

But the roots of the teaching about the Shechinah lie in something more than this Fatherhood idea.   The Kingdom idea must be reckoned with—the Kingdom of Heaven, as it is familiarly designated both in the Rabbinic literature and in the Prayer-book of the Synagogue.   As in the case of the Fatherhood, so here, too, we must seek the origin of the Kingdom in the compass of the Old Testament.   In the latter, the kingship of God is sometimes pictured as an event consummated in the present and sometimes as some ' far-off divine event ' in the remote future.   Thus *Psalm,* cxlv. 13, says :   " Thy kingdom is an everlasting kingdom, and thy dominion endureth throughout all generations."   This is clearly a *present* kingship. *Zechariah,* xiv. 9, says :   " And the Lord shall be king over the whole earth, on that day shall he be one and his name one."   This is obviously a future kingship.

The student of Apocryphal and Apocalyptic literature will find it bearing the same duality of meaning there too.   In the Rabbinic literature it is further amplified. The favourite expression there is ' the taking upon one's self [or the receiving] of the yoke of the Kingdom of Heaven.' An examination of several of the contexts in which the phrase is embedded, proves that it stands for a conglomeration of doctrines, such as that : (*a*) The Jew must abandon idolatry (*i.e.* servitude to man or the work of man's hands). (*b*) He must desire and work for the universal recognition of the Jewish God. (*c*) He must acknowledge and feel the ' nearness ' of God to him, the Divine companionship ever enshrouding him and his race, the direct revelation of a living and loving God in all fields of his activity and hope. (*d*) The Jew must acknowledge himself as one of a band, and not as an isolated unit—a band held and welded together by the feeling that it is a kingdom within a Kingdom—a greater Kingdom, the Kingdom of Heaven. The so-called ' clannishness ' of the Jews, their tendency for herding together, a fault for which they are continuously scolded, abused or, at best, derided, is thus seen to be based upon a motive which is by no means as undesirable as it is generally pictured to be. The Jewish flock must be one because the ' kingdom ' of the Jews must be one—and the latter ' kingdom ' must be one because the ' Kingdom of Heaven ' in which it is comprised and which thrills it through and informs it, is one. " God is king in Jeshurun," say the sages (in allusion to their particular interpretation of

Deuteronomy, xxxiii. 5), only when "the heads of the people are assembled, and the tribes of Israel are together." In other words, the earthly kingdom is the *fons et origo* of the Heavenly. Remove the earthly kingdom and you remove the Divine Revelation of God in the midst of Israel. The Heavenly Kingdom is broken up and vanishes. Its *raison d'être* is completely gone.

For the individual Jew there are two avenues along which the Kingdom of Heaven can be brought in and consolidated. These are : (*a*) as already said, by his harbouring an intense sense of the solidarity of his race ; (*b*) by prayer. A remarkable passage, in *T.B. Berachoth*, 10b, runs thus : " Whosoever eats and drinks previous to praying, of him it is said, ' And me hast thou cast behind thy back ' (1 *Kings*, xiv. 9). Do not read ' thy back ' (*gey-vĕ-kāh*) but read ' thy pride ' (*gey-ĕ-kāh*), *i.e.* after priding himself (with food and drink) this man thinks to take upon himself the Kingdom of Heaven."

These two conceptions already described, *viz.* (*a*) the abounding, manifested love involved in Fatherhood, combined with (*b*) the incorporation of a Heavenly Kingdom within the folds of an Israel welded in strictest fellowship, these two conceptions lie at the root of the mysticism of the Shechinah.

' Shechinah ' comes from *shachan* = to dwell. The whole edifice of thought about the Shechinah is based upon such passages in the Old Testament as " And let them make me a sanctuary that I may dwell among them " (*Exodus*, xxv. 8). " Defile ye not therefore the land which ye shall inhabit, wherein I dwell : for I the Lord dwell among the children of Israel;" (*Numbers*, xxxv. 34). " And I will set my tabernacle among you and my soul shall not abhor you. And I will walk among you and will be your God, and ye shall be my people " (*Leviticus*, xxvi. 11, 12).

The Israelites were one compact fellowship, an indivisible organism, and not a series of separate units. God's dwelling among them, or placing His Tabernacle among them in Old Testament times, was interpreted by the Rabbis of the Talmud and Midrashim as implying that there is a permanent presence of the Divine Spirit in the midst of the people of Israel ; and that this Divine Spirit not only accompanies them without ceasing, but that it also imparts itself, communicates itself, to every member of Israel whenever he orders his life in such a way as to be capable of realising it. It is a perpetual incoming of the Divine Life into the human life of the Jew. It is a " Divine-human fellowship which only fails when the human partner [the people of Israel] is in sin." Israel is bathed in a Divine environment. As the great mystic theologian

among the Jews of the middle ages (Moses
Naḥmanides, born in Spain 1194, died in
Palestine about 1270) says, in commenting
on *Leviticus*, xxvi. 11 : " The Divine soul, of
which His dwelling among us is a part, will
not thrust us forth [when we work and live
aright] as a vessel when heated by hot water
thrusts forth its impurities."

All this is meant by the Shechinah.
Writers on mysticism, no matter to what
school of religious thought they may happen
to belong, familiarise us with the great fact
that the mystic, by reason of the high levels
of spiritual intensity on which his life is
lived, experiences certain physical sensations
which enable him to *see* or to *hear* something
of the mystery of the Divine Presence.
Christian mysticism invariably quotes the
experiences of Paul in this connection—
Paul who was so deeply struck by the
brilliant light about him that he " was three
days without sight and neither did eat nor
drink " (*Acts*, ix. 9).   Evelyn Underhill says
of a certain mediæval German mystic,
Rulman Merswin, that " a brilliant light
shone around him ; he heard in his ears
a Divine voice of adorable sweetness ; he
felt as if he were lifted from the ground,
and carried several times round the garden "
(*The Mystic Way*, p. 162).

Phenomena of a similar type cluster round
the Shechinah mysticism.   Thus, a passage

in *Leviticus Rabba*, xx. 10, commenting
on *Exodus*, xxiv. ("And upon the nobles of
the children of Israel he laid not his hand;
also they saw God, and did eat and drink"),
runs thus: "R. Tanḥuma said that this
verse teaches us that they [*i.e.* the nobles of
Israel] uncovered their heads and made their
hearts swell with pride and feasted their eyes
on the Shechinah. . . . But Moses did not
feast his eyes on the Shechinah, and yet he
gained a benefit from the Shechinah [*viz.*
that 'the skin of his face shone' (*Exodus*,
xxxiv. 35)]."

Three points are noteworthy here.
Firstly, the *strongly materialised* characterisation of the Shechinah. It was actually a
physical food to the onlookers. Secondly,
the physical impressions created by the sight
of it. The uncovering of the head was no
trivial bodily movement. Involving as it
did a distinct breach of the oriental mode
of showing veneration to a superior, it
must have been a highly purposeful act.
Thirdly, the contrast between the experience
of Moses and that of the nobles is intended
to bring out what is a cardinal feature of
the Shechinah mysticism, *viz.* that in
spite of the fact that the Shechinah is the
Presence inseparable from Israel, accompanying him whithersoever he goes, yet the
realisation of this Presence by the individual
Israelite can only come after a series of

spiritual and moral disciplinary acts of the highest order have been gone through by him.

Thus said the Rabbis, the Shechinah says of the proud man : " There is no room for this man and myself in the world." Again : " Whosoever commits a sin in secret acts as though he were pressing against the feet of the Shechinah, as it is said (*Isaiah,* lxvi. 1), ' Thus saith the Lord, the heavens are my throne and the earth is my footstool ' " (*T.B. Kiddūshin,* 31a). " Whosoever shows anger regards the Shechinah as though it were a thing of nought " (*T.B. Nedarim,* 22b). " The Shechinah only resides with him who is at once wise, strong and wealthy " (*T.B. Sabbath,* 92a)— ' wise ' denoting the perfection of spirituality; ' strong ' denoting the perfection of the physical faculties;[1] ' wealthy ' standing for the perfection of the moral qualities, because, as the Rabbis explained, the man of wealth being independent of the smiles and favours of his fellow-men, will not readily fall a prey to that great perverter of morals —the sin of accepting bribes.

Other instances of the way in which the Shechinah was objectivised and experienced through the channels of the visual or auditory

---

[1] The Rabbis (in *T.B. Nedarim,* 38a) give some curious illustrations of Moses' wealth, strength and wisdom—all deduced from Old Testament verses.

senses are the following: " The Shechinah
used to beat before Samson like a bell "
(*T.B. Soṭah*, 9b). This is a commentary on
Judges, xiii. 25, " And the Spirit of the Lord
began to move him " (the Hebrew word for
' to move ' is here from the same root as the
Hebrew word for a ' bell '). In *Canticles
Rabba*, ii., the Shechinah is visible from
between the shoulders and fingers of the
priests at the time they pronounce upon
Israel the priestly benediction of *Numbers*,
vi. 24–26 : " The Lord bless thee and keep
thee ; the Lord make his face shine upon
thee, and be gracious unto thee ; the Lord
lift up his countenance upon thee and give
thee peace." [1]

In the Midrash *Tanḥuma* on chapter xvi.
of *Leviticus*, the Shechinah is associated with
the sense of smell—another phenomenon of
the mystic life much dwelt upon by modern
writers on the subject. Aaron's rod is stated

[1] Philo says : " For what life can be better than that which
is devoted to speculation, or what can be more closely
connected with rational existence ? For which reason it is
that though the voices of mortal beings are judged of by
the faculty of hearing, nevertheless the Scriptures present to
us the words of God to be actually visible to us like light ;
for in them it is said that, ' All the people *saw* the voice of
God ' (*Exodus*, xx. 18) ; they do not say ' heard ' it, since
what took place was not a beating of the air by means of
the organs of the mouth and tongue, but a most exceedingly
brilliant ray of virtue not different in any respect from the
source of reason, which also in another passage is spoken of
in the following manner, ' Ye have seen that I spake unto
you from out of heaven ' (*ibid.* 22), not ' Ye have heard ' for
the same reason " (On the *Migration of Abraham*, ix.).

to have 'smelt the Shechinah.' Similarly in
the *Yalkut* on *Canticles*, i., a mystical inference
is drawn from the usage of the metaphor of
'a bundle of myrrh' applied to 'my well-
beloved,' *i.e.* God.

In *T.B. Megillah*, 29a, it is stated as follows:
" The father of Samuel and Levi [Babylonian
Rabbis of the 3rd century A.D.] were once
sitting in the synagogue of Shef-Ve-Yatib in
Nehardea [Babylon]. They suddenly heard
a sound of movement. *It was the Shechinah
coming.* They at once rose and went out.
A fellow-Rabbi by name Shesheth (who was
blind) was once sitting in the same synagogue,
and when the Shechinah came, he did not go
out. Then the ministering angels came and
struck terror into him." In the end Shesheth
addresses the Shechinah, who advises the
angels to cease from vexing him.

It must be borne in mind, in this connection,
how intimately conjoined, in the minds of the
Rabbis, was the idea 'synagogue' with the
idea 'Shechinah.' The blending of the two
even went so far as to prompt the Rabbis to
say—what is sometimes falsely and foolishly
described as 'grotesque'—that God prays
and the synagogue is His house of prayer.
Hence if it is true, as Evelyn Underhill
maintains, that the visionary experience of
mystics is 'a picture which the mind constructs . . . from raw materials already at
its disposal' (*Mysticism*, p. 325), one can

quite see how the consciousness of being inside the synagogue should bring home to the Rabbi, in so particularly drastic a fashion, the reality of the Shechinah's intercourse with men.

Noteworthy also—and this is, as well, one of the distinguishing features of the mystical temperament—is the contrast in the effects which this sudden invasion of a Divine Presence had upon the objects of the visitation. The two Rabbis who left the synagogue did so, most probably, as the result of the fearful weakening and depressing effect of the vision. The Rabbi, however, who stayed on and succeeded in eliciting from the Shechinah a promise that the ministering angels should henceforth cease from troubling him, is the type of the mystic who feels the mental and physical elation, the joy, the rapture, the triumph consequent upon the conviction of his having, at last, reached the goal of his quest—the sight, sound and touch of the Ultimate Reality.

A feature of the Shechinah mysticism which deserves a deeper appreciation than is usually accorded it, is to be found in the reiterated Rabbinic belief that goodness and piety radiate an atmosphere of divinity which infects all who breathe it, with a new impulse towards the good, the beautiful and the true. The good man can bring the Shechinah to his fellows. He can invest earth with the quality which belongs to Heaven. Sight of, or contact with, a saint, is equivalent to an inflowing of the Shechinah. Thus, a striking passage in *Canticles Rabba,* vi., says :

" The original abode of the Shechinah was among the ' *taḥtonim,*' *i.e.* the lower ones, *i.e.* human beings, earth. When Adam sinned, it ascended away to the first heaven. With Cain's sin, it ascended to the second ; with Enoch's, to the third ; with the generation of the Flood, to the fourth ; with the generation of the Tower of Babel, to the fifth ; with the Sodomites, to the sixth. With the sin of the Egyptians in the days of Abraham, it ascended to the seventh. Corresponding to these there arose seven righteous men who brought the Shechinah down back to earth again. These were Abraham, Isaac, Jacob, Kehath, Amram, and Moses."

There is, of course, a strong sprinkling of the ' fellowship ' idea which, as was said on a previous page, is a basic factor in Jewish spirituality. The greater the bond of union between the members of the Jewish brotherhood, the greater the realisation of the Divine Presence in their midst. Add to this the existence of men of conspicuous piety within the bosom of the fellowship, and you have all the essentials for a deeper and stronger infiltration of the Divine stream. The

Shechinah is brought back to men by the aid of the better men.

The same train of thought is expressed more pointedly by the following aphorisms :

T.B. Berachoth, 64, says : "Whosoever partakes of a meal at which a ' disciple of the wise ' is present, it is as though he enjoyed of the splendour of the Shechinah." Clearly, the presence of the ' disciple of the wise ' makes the life of the company about him to be lived on higher levels. He gives it an access to the Divine which it would not otherwise [have had. *T.B. Ketuboth*, 105a, says : "Whosoever brings a gift to a ' disciple of the wise ' it is as though he brought the first-fruits (*bikkurim*) to the Temple." The ' disciple of the wise ' is here a Temple in human form. To approach him is to approach a Holy of Holies. Contact with him is a sanctifying influence. He radiates divinity.

T.B. Ketuboth, 111b, says : "Is it possible for any man to cling to the Shechinah ? For is it not said, in *Deuteronomy*, iv. 24, ' For the Lord thy God is a consuming fire ' ? But the meaning is this : Whosoever marries his daughter to a ' disciple of the wise ' or engages in any enterprise with him, or who lets a ' disciple of the wise ' enjoy of his worldly possessions, it is counted unto him, by Holy Writ, as though he clung to the Shechinah."

Companionship with the good must be acquired at all costs. It is the dynamic power for opening the door to the spiritual world. The man of virtue is Shechinah-possessed ; and to touch only the hem of his garment is to become Shechinah-possessed too.

When Ruth the Moabitess forsakes her ancestral gods in favour of the God of Israel, when Abram, according to the Rabbinic interpretation of *Genesis,* xii. 5 (' And the souls that they had gotten in Harran '), brings the weary and footsore into his home and initiates them into the belief in the God in whom he himself believes, the Rabbis say that the act performed in both cases is ' the entering of the non-Israelite under the wings of the Shechinah.'

The narrow, exclusive nationalist view of the Deity is very apparent in these and many other similar utterances. The Shechinah is for Israel only. The Shechinah is primarily for Israel. God is near to the Jew, far from the non-Jew. These are seemingly natural and correct deductions from the Rabbinic records. If so, is not the term ' mysticism ' as applied to the Shechinah a misnomer, seeing that the primal assumption of mysticism is the truth that *every* soul, notwithstanding race or religion, can have intimate intercourse with the Divine ? The answer is this :

The title ' Jew ' or ' Israelite ' is frequently

used by the Rabbis in a more comprehensive
sense than they are usually given credit for.
Thus *T.B. Kiddushin*, 40a, says : " Whosoever denies the truth of idolatry becomes a
believer in the whole Torah." *T.B. Megillah*,
13a, says : " Whosoever denies idolatry is
called a Jew." In the Midrash *Sifra* on
Leviticus, xvi. there is a comment on *Psalm*,
cxxv. 4, " Do good, O Lord, unto those that
be good, and to them that are upright in
their heart." " The Psalmist," says the
Sifra, " does *not* say ' Do good to the
Priests or to the Levites or to the Israelites.'
But he says ' Do good unto those that be
good.' " More instances could be quoted
did space not forbid.

From the first of the quotations just given,
it follows that ' Jew ' is a term of the widest
scope. From the second one infers that the
Jew fills no higher a place in the Divine favour
than do the good and worthy of all men and
races.

" Yea, He loveth the people," says the
Deuteronomist (xxxiii. 3). " Yes," says
Rabbi Samuel b. Meir, the great Rabbinic
commentator of the 12th century, " God
loveth also the nations of the world." Of
King Solomon's chariot it is said (*Canticles*,
iii. 10) that " the midst thereof is paved with
love." " This love in the midst thereof,"
say the Rabbis, " is the Shechinah." It is
certainly not meant in any sectarian sense.

The Divine Chariot in Jewish mysticism is, broadly, the idealised universe. And all degrees of creation from amœba to man hold and reveal the traces of the Divine love which is ever born anew in our hearts and which guarantees the ultimate goodness of the world.

CHAPTER V

THE date and origin of this extraordinary book—the oldest philosophical work in the Hebrew language—are shrouded in obscurity. There is as yet no critical edition of it, although there are several translations of it, both of the whole and of parts, into Latin, German, and French; and the numerous commentaries written on it in Arabic and Hebrew (and the subsequent translations of these into Latin, German, etc.) show, not only the high position which it held in the estimation of Jewish thinkers from the 10th century onward, but also the great influence which it wielded on the general development of Jewish mystical speculation.

The difficulties of fixing its date and origin are illustrated by the fact that whereas the voice of mediæval Jewish scholarship assigned its -authorship to the patriarch Abraham (on the grounds of some supposed internal evidence), individual writers here and there credited the book to Rabbi 'Akiba

THE BOOK 'YETSIRAH'   99

(50–130 A.D.)—'Akiba having been an adept
in the mystic lore of numbers; and the
Book *Yetsirah* is pervaded with the mystical
significances of numbers. Others, again,
without touching the question of authorship,
give it an origin in the late Talmudic epoch—
about the 6th century A.D. This theory is
the likeliest of all, because the 6th century
marks the beginning of what is known in
Jewish history as the Gaonic epoch, when
several Rabbinic-mystical works, second in
importance only to the Book *Yetsirah,* were
composed.

The latest theory is that of Reitzenstein
(*Poimandres,* pp. 14, 56, 261, 291) who,
arguing from the resemblances between the
doctrines of letters and numbers in this book
and the miraculous cosmic powers wielded by
numbers and letters in the thaumaturgical
books current among the Gnostics of the
2nd century B.C., concludes that it is a
Hebrew production of the 2nd century B.C.
The fatal objection to Reitzenstein's theory,
however, seems to lie in the fact that his
argument holds good of only one aspect of
the work, *viz.* the philological part. The
other part — the philosophical — although
vitally connected with the philological and
deduced from it — contains elements of
thought and modes of expression which are
many centuries later than the pre-Christian
Gnosticism. But Reitzenstein's theory cuts

very deeply and cannot be disposed of in a few words.

The clue to the particular nature of the Book *Yetsirah* lies in its two constituent elements which we have a moment ago contrasted. It is a mystical philosophy drawn from the sounds, shapes, relative positions, and numerical values of the letters of the Hebrew alphabet. The nucleus of much of this teaching is to be found in the Talmud, but the Rabbis were certainly not the originators of it. Just as Philo excelled in the art of clothing Grecian philosophy in a Hebraic dress, so did the Rabbis show a considerable capacity for ' naturalising ' many an alien product. In the case of the mysticism under consideration they drew from older available sources — Egyptian, Babylonian, Mandæan—and adapted the idea to the framework of their own essential lore.

Thus in *T.B. Berachoth*, 55a, there occurs the remark, " Bezaleel [the architect of the Tabernacle in the desert] knew how to join together (*lĕ-tsa-rĕf*) the letters by means of which the heavens and earth were created." This is because he was " filled with the spirit of God, with wisdom and understanding " (*Exodus*, xxxi. 3), and this wisdom is the same as that of *Proverbs*, iii. 19 : " The Lord by wisdom founded the earth." This belief in the magic power of the letters of the alphabet can be traced to Zoroastrianism and ultimately to Chaldea —as Lenormant has shown in his *Chaldean Magic.* It was by means of the combination of letters comprising the Holy Name of God that the disciples of Judah the Prince (*c.* 135–220 A.D.), who were keen on cosmogony, used to create a three-year-old calf on the eve of every Sabbath and used to eat it on the Sabbath. So says a passage in *T.B. Sanhedrin,* 65b. There is a strong flavour of old Semitic witchcraft here. It is an *exotic* notion introduced for the purpose of intensifying an essentially Jewish belief —the belief in the wonder-working powers bestowed by the Sabbath on those who scrupulously uphold it. The practice of magic and witchcraft was sternly reprobated by the Old Testament, and the Rabbis were equally severe in its condemnation.

One quotation from the book will suffice to give us a glimpse into the supernatural importance of the forms, sounds, and relative positions of the letters in the Hebrew alphabet. It says : " Twenty-two letters : He drew them, hewed them, combined them, weighed them, interchanged them, and through them produced the whole creation and everything that is destined to come into being " (ii. 2). Each of the actions here mentioned, *viz.* ' drawing,' ' hewing,' ' combining,' ' weighing,' ' interchanging,' is de-

scribed with a fulness which is as bizarre
as it is bewildering ; and although the interest is mainly a philological one, it is an
indispensable part of the book's philosophy.

As it would be impossible to give the
reader any tangible notion of these involved
stretches of philological reasoning, without
introducing a considerable amount of Hebrew
words and Hebrew grammatical terminology,
the subject can only be dealt with fragmentarily. The letters of the Hebrew alphabet
are pressed into the service of a doctrine
which is an element of ancient Semitic
theosophy, and which passed thence into
Greek philosophy. It is the doctrine of the
three primordial substances—water, fire, and
air. These three substances underlie all
creation, and are the fountain-head of all
existence. The three Hebrew letters playing the principal part in connection with
these three primal substances are Aleph
(א), Mem (מ), and Shin (ש). Why just these
letters ? For two reasons.

Firstly, these three letters represent three
cardinal divisions into which the twenty-two
letters of the Hebrew alphabet naturally fall.
The divisions are : (*a*) mutes unaccompanied
by any sound in producing them (as can be
seen by any one who tries the pronunciation
of the sound of Mem—it is merely a com-
pression of the lips); (*b*) sibilants, best
represented by Shin ; (*c*) aspirates, the class

to which Aleph belongs—this class being, in
the naïve imagination of these theosophists,
intermediate to the mutes and the sibilants
and, as it were, holding the balance between
them. Hence these three letters are called
' mothers ' (*ĕm* = mother) because all the
other letters are, as it were, born from them.
The mediæval Kabbalah, as will be mentioned
later on, likewise speaks of ' father ' and
' mother ' in somewhat similar connections.

Secondly, these three representative
' parent ' letters—the mute, the sibilant, the
aspirate—symbolise the three basic elements
of all existing things, the three primordial
substances. Thus water (the first letter of
which word in Hebrew is Mem) is symbolised
by the mute Mem. Why ? Because the
chief product of water is fish ; and fish are
the representatives of the mute creation.
Fire (in Hebrew *esh*, most prominent in
pronunciation is *sh*) is symbolised by the
sibilant Shin. Why ? Because the characteristic of fire is its hissing sound ; and
the equivalent in Hebrew for ' sibilant ' is a
word which means ' hissing.' Air (the first
letter of which word in Hebrew is Aleph) is
symbolised by the aspirate Aleph, which has
an airy, vacant pronunciation. Just as
Aleph holds the balance between the mute
letters and the sibilants, so air is, in the
natural world, intermediate to the water
which always tends in a downward direction,

and fire which by its nature always ascends.
Of course it needs no hard reasoning here to
see how an alien system of very early thought
has been mechanically and arbitrarily foisted
on to the Hebrew alphabet.

But, as was before mentioned, all the
twenty-two letters of the Hebrew alphabet
play a dominant *rôle* in the book's philosophy.
Thus we read (ii. 2) :

" By means of the twenty-two letters, by
giving them a form and a shape, by mixing
them and combining them in different ways,
God made the soul of all that which has been
created and of all that which will be.   It is
upon these same letters that the Holy One
(blessed be He) has founded B is high and holy
Name."

This remark probably indicates that the
existence of these letters and the impress
which they leave in every particle of creation
are the unfailing source of our knowledge of
that supreme Intelligence which, while being
immanent in the universe, is its guide and
controller and holds all the different parts
together.   In short, the harmony of the
cosmos is due to the Divine wisdom underlying
the manipulations of the twenty-two letters.

These twenty-two letters are split up into
three divisions.   These are : (i.) The three
which have just been considered, the three
' mothers ' or ' parent ' letters (Aleph, Mem,
Shin) which symbolise the elements, air,

fire, and water, which together make up the cosmos. The year (or time), which is part of the cosmos, also consists of three parts—three seasons, *viz.* summer, which corresponds to the element fire ; winter, which corresponds to the element water ; spring and autumn, which form a season intermediate to the other two, correspond to the element air, which also is intermediate to the fire and the water. Again, the human body is likewise a trinity, composed of head, chest, and stomach, and likewise corresponds to the three elements. And the world is a trinity too. Fire is the substance of the heavens, water (condensed) is the basis of earth, air is the dividing medium necessary for preserving the peace between the two.

(ii.) The seven double letters typify the ' contraries ' in the cosmos, the forces which serve two mutually opposed ends. Thus, there are seven planets which exercise at times a good and at times a bad influence upon men and things. There are seven days in the week ; but there are also seven nights. And so on. It is all arbitrary and highly dubious. The seven ' double ' letters are Beth, Gimel, Daleth, Caph, Pĕh, Resh, Tau. They are ' double ' because they express two different sounds according as they possess *dagesh* or not. The letter Resh is not usually classed among these by Hebrew grammarians. By deducting these seven and the

three ' parent ' letters, we get the remaining
twelve ' simple ' letters.

(iii.) The twelve ' simple ' letters are em-
blematic of the twelve signs of the zodiac,
the twelve months of the year, the twelve
organs in the human body which perform
their work independently of the outside world
and are subject to the twelve signs of the
zodiac. A strong Gnostic colouring pervades
the whole.

Thus the cosmos—embraced ideally in the
twenty-two letters—is an expression of the
Divine Intelligence. Man, the world, time—
these three constitute the cosmos, and outside them there is but one great existence, the
Infinite.

This brings us to two doctrines of Jewish
mysticism which appear for the first time
in the Book *Yetsirah*, and which were developed subsequently on diverse lines. These
are : (*a*) the doctrine of emanation ; (*b*)
the Ten Sefirot.

In the general literature of mysticism, the
doctrine (or rather doctrines) of emanation is
usually associated for the first time with the
great name of Plotinus (born at Lycopolis,
in Egypt, about 205 A.D.). This remark
raises a twofold reflection which is of the
highest interest. Firstly, it shows how one
particularly influential aspect of mysticism,
viz. emanation, is a feature common to the
theologies of both the early Church and the

early Synagogue—sundered as these two were
from one another by so many other irrecon-
cilable points of disagreement. Secondly,
it shows how both Jewish and Christian
mysticism are alike indebted to one and the
same set of sources, *viz.* Gnosticism and its
development—the Alexandrian Neoplatonism. The latter is the pith and core of
the emanation doctrines of Plotinus. It is
equally the root of the emanation doctrines
of the Book *Yetsirah*, the *Zohar*, and, in
fact, all branches of the mediæval Kabbalah.

Emanation implies that all existing things
are successive outflowings or outgoings of
God. God contains within Himself all. He
is perfect, incomprehensible, indivisible, dependent on nothing, in need of nothing.
Everything in the cosmos, all finite creatures
animate and inanimate, flow out, radiate, in
a successive series, from God, the Perfect
One. The *motif* of this teaching is that of
explaining the difficulties involved in the
inevitable assumption of all religion, *viz.*
that there is a bond of relationship between
God and His creation. How can there be
any connecting link between a Being who is
self-sufficient, unchangeable, infinite, perfect,
and matter which is finite, changeable, imperfect, etc. ? This is the difficulty. All
doctrines of emanation answer it in more or
less the same way, by saying that God is
not really external to any one or anything.

Everything is originally comprehended in Him, " with no contrasts of here or there, no oppositions of this and that, no separation into change and variation " (Rufus Jones, *Studies in Mystical Religion*, p. 73).   On this understanding there is no necessity for hunting after ' the missing link ' between the Divine and the human.   The multiplicity that one beholds in the cosmos, the whole panorama of thought, action, goodness, badness, the soul, the mind—all things that go to make up the pageant of man's life in the universe, are emanations, radiations from the one Unity, manifestations of the God from whom all things flow and to whom they must all finally return because they are ultimately one with the One, just as the flame is one with the candle from which it issues.

In the Book *Yetsirah,* the teaching about emanation is intertwined with the doctrine of the Ten Sefirot.   The object of this intertwining is that of giving a more decidedly *Jewish* colouring to the Neoplatonic conceptions of emanations.   The Jewish mystics, however far they may have wandered into other fields for their views about God, always felt that the *Hebrew Bible and God as preached by the Hebrew Bible* must be the core of their message.   There, thought they, lies the final Truth.   Final Truth, taught they, is but a commentary on the Hebrew Bible.

Where did the idea of the Sefirot originate ?

In all probability it originated with the Rabbis of the Talmud in the first three centuries of the Christian era. Thus, a passage in *T.B. Ḥaggigah*, 12a, speaks of the "Ten agencies through which God created the world, *viz.* wisdom, insight, cognition, strength, power, inexorableness, justice, right, love, mercy."

There are, as will be shown more fully in a later chapter, some obvious resemblances between these ten creative potentialities of the Talmud, and the Ten Sefirot of our Book and of the mediæval Kabbalah (though the resemblances between those of the Talmud and of the Kabbalah are considerably stronger than the resemblances between those of the Talmud and our Book *Yetsirah*). To these facts must be added also the personification of Wisdom as well as of Torah by the early Rabbis, and their doctrine about the creation of the world by two *Middot* (Attributes), *viz.* the Attribute of Mercy and the Attribute of Justice.

Let us turn to the description of the Ten Sefirot as given by the Book *Yetsirah* (i. 9):

"There are Ten Sefirot—ten, not nine; ten, not eleven. Act in order to understand them in thy wisdom and thy intelligence; so that thy investigations exercise themselves continually upon them; also thy speculations, thy knowledge, thy thought, thy imagination; make things to rest upon their principle and re-establish the Creator upon his foundation."

Again (i. 3) :

" The Ten Sefirot are like the fingers of the hand, ten in number, five corresponding to five. But in the middle of them is the knot of the Unity."

There is a tantalising vagueness about these descriptions, and, as modern scholars always hasten to point out, the Sefirot of the Book *Yetsirah* differ from those of the *Zohar* and the mediæval Kabbalah generally in one cardinal respect, *viz.* that whereas in the two latter systems the Sefirot have the fullest possible mystical connotation, in the *Yetsirah* Book they cluster mainly round the mysticism of numbers. Numbers and letters (of the Hebrew alphabet, as we have seen) give the main impetus to the peculiar teaching. Divine action in its relation to the universe is conceived in the form of abstract numbers. But yet the following quotation from the book shows a clear foreshadowing of a real mystical system such as is seen in the *Zohar*.

" The first of the Sefirot, *one,* is the spirit (*Ruaḥ*) of the living God (blessed be His Name, blessed be the Name of Him who inhabits eternity !). The spirit, the voice, and the word, these are the Holy Spirit."

The second of the Sefirot, *two,* is the air which comes from the spirit. On it are hewn and engraven the twenty-two letters which form altogether but one breath.

The third of the Sefirot, *three*, is the water which comes from the air [*i.e.* condensed vapour]. It is in the water that He has dug the darknesses and the chaos, that He has formed the earth and the clay, which was spread out afterwards in the form of a carpet, hewn out like a wall and covered as though by a roof.

The fourth of the Sefirot, *four*, is the fire which comes from the water, and with which He has made the throne of His glory, the heavenly Ophanim (Wheels), the Seraphim, and the ministering angels. With the three together He has built his dwelling, as it is written, "He maketh the winds his messengers, his ministers a flaming fire" (*Psalm*, civ. 4).

The remaining six Sefirot are the six dimensions of space—the four cardinal points of the compass, in addition to height and depth.

The difficulties here are many, and some are insuperable. Are the Sefirot really a piece of Jewish mysticism (as was suggested before) or are they nothing more than echoes of the Gnostic systems of number-manipulations?

What is the relation between the cosmic powers of the twenty-two letters of the Hebrew alphabet and the cosmic powers of the Sefirot?

What bearing has the doctrine of the three
primal elements upon the first four Sefirot
which seem to contain very much the same
thought ?

In the answer to the first of these queries
lies the clue to the nature of the book.   The
Book *Yetsirah* is syncretic, and while the
emphasised significance of the number ' ten,'
as well as the importance of the idea of the
world as the scene of Divine Agencies (or
Middot), is in its native origin Jewish, the
teaching about the creative powers of
letters and numbers is only Jewish by
adoption, and whether the word ' Sefirot ' is
originally Jewish or alien is a moot point ;
the notion of the three primal substances is
clearly an exotic foisted on to the book to
give it the appearance of the philosophic
completeness which the age demanded.
Viewing the book, therefore, as a mosaic
rather than a concrete and continuous whole,
it is futile to ask questions about the con-
sistency of its parts.   What, however, we
can do, and ought to do, is to try to see how
the author pieced his mosaic together so as
to give to his readers what, in his opinion,
was a presentation of the doctrine of emanation as interpreted by the spirit of Judaism.

It will be noticed that the three primal
substances, air, fire, water, are identical with
the second, third, and fourth of the Sefirot,
but whereas each of these is produced from

the preceding one, the three primal substances seem to be all independent of one
another as regards production. And again,
the second, third, and fourth of the Sefirot
all emanate originally from the first, *viz.*
the *Ruaḥ*—the Spirit of the living God. No
such notion attaches to the three primal substances. The object in all this seems to be
that of giving an essentially Jewish colouring
to cosmogony. Everything was brought
forth by the Spirit of God. As the Psalmist
says : " By the word of the Lord were the
heavens made; and all the host of them by
the breath of his mouth " (xxxiii. 6). It is
a counterblast to the Aristotelian doctrine
of the eternity of matter which to the Jewish
mediæval mind was rank blasphemy. To
say that everything emanates originally from
the Spirit of God is tantamount to the asser-
tion that the prototypes of matter are all of
them aspects or modifications of the Divine
Spirit. This, again, is to put a more Jewish
complexion on the doctrine of emanation,
which, when carried out to its logical conclusion in the philosophy of Neoplatonism,
leads to pantheism—another pitfall which
our author apparently wanted to avoid.

That such a construction is a tenable one
is seen from the book's remark, " The last of
the Sefirot unites itself to its first just like
a flame is joined to the candle, for God is
one and there is no second " (i. 5). The

offence of recognising 'two Divine powers' (*shêté-rĕ-shooyôt*) was always a terrible one to the Jewish mind. Again, all the numbers from two to ten are derived from the unit, one. Even so does all the multiplicity and variety of forms, types, etc., in the cosmos find its highest consummation, its ultimate home and goal, in the Unity, *viz.* God. Here, again, we see how an alien system of number-mysticism is drafted into the fold of an essentially Jewish type of mysticism, *viz.* that clustering round the cardinal notion of the Unity of God. This theme, after being elaborated by the Talmudic Rabbis of the opening centuries of Christianity, was again taken up by the mediæval Jewish theologians, and reached the zenith of its mystical development in the pages of the *Zohar* and the mediæval Kabbalah generally.

But what is the relation between the cosmic powers of the twenty-two letters of the Hebrew alphabet and the cosmic parts played by the Ten Sefirot? The answer would seem to lie in the peculiar description which the book itself, in one place, gives to the Sefirot. The latter are, it says, 'Ten Sefirot without anything' (*bêlēē mā*). In other words 'abstracts.' They are the categories of the universe, the forms or moulds into which all created things were originally cast. They are *form*, as distinguished from matter. Whereas the Sefirot are responsible

for the first production of form, so the twenty-
two letters are the prime cause of matter.
All existence and development are due to
the creative powers of the letters, but they
are inconceivable apart from the *form* with
which the Sefirot has invested them.

The Book *Yetsirah* lands us into the heart
of Jewish mysticism and prepares the way
for the ramified literature of the *Zohar*. It
does this by teaching that God and the world
are a unity rather than a dualism. The
Sefirot and the twenty-two letters of the
alphabet, or, in other words, the forms and
essences which make up the visible universe,
are all an unfolding of the Divine, all
emanations from the Spirit. God is at one
and the same time both the matter and form
of the universe. But He is something more.
He is not identical with the universe. He
is greater than it, transcends it. Nothing
exists or can exist outside Him. Though
immanent, He is also and at the same time
transcendent. This insistence upon the
Divine transcendence runs like a golden
thread throughout all branches of Jewish
mysticism, thus enabling it, both as a system
of thought and as a phase of practical
religion, to do justice at once to the ' legal '
and spiritual elements which are inextricably
intertwined in Judaism.

But if the Book *Yetsirah* gave the impulse
to the great books of mediæval Jewish

mysticism, it was eclipsed by them in one great particular. The naïve conception of the mysterious powers of letters and numbers was superseded by the introduction of theological and moral ideas. The object of discussion became not so much the relationship between the Creator and His cosmos as the relationship between God and that inner surging world of thought and emotion which we term man. How man can ascend to God whilst bound in the trammels of the flesh or after having shuffled off this ' muddy vesture of decay,' how God communicates Himself to man, imparting to him the knowledge which has its fountain-head in His own inexhaustible Being and the love which is the seal of His abiding goodness and nearness,— these themes form, roughly speaking, the staple of the *Zohar* mysticism which presents itself for brief consideration in the coming pages.

CHAPTER VI

SOME GENERAL FEATURES OF THE 'ZOHAR' MYSTICISM

THE *Zohar* (lit. = 'Shining' or 'Brightness' from the word in *Daniel,* xii. 3—" And they that be wise shall shine as the brightness of the firmament ") is, *par excellence*, the text-book of Jewish mediæval mysticism. Its language is partly Aramaic and partly Hebrew. While purporting to be but a commentary on the Pentateuch, it is, in reality, quite an independent compendium of Kabbalistic theosophy. Its style, its subject-matter, its spirit lead the reader into realms which bear hardly any conceivable resemblance to the manner and substance of the Pentateuch.

The *Zohar* compares well with the Talmud in one respect. They are both painfully unsystematic in the handling of their sub-ject-matter. Both present us with a bizarre medley of ideas and facts, an ill-assorted conglomeration of history and fable, truth and fiction, serious comment which has a value for all time and observations which

the march of time asks us to dismiss as
outworn and valueless. Both works, too,
cover a long stretch of time.

The *Zohar* is a pseudepigraphic work.
It is impossible, in the present book, to give
the reader even the faintest outlines of the
literature written by Jews of many countries
and many centuries, on the vexed question
of the authorship of the *Zohar*. It pretends
to be the record of a direct Divine revelation
to Rabbi Simeon ben Yoḥai (born in Galilee
2nd century A.D.); and it is mainly written in
the form of a series of utterances from the
mouth of Simeon to his disciples, who believed him to be conveying to them the
truths which he had received first-hand from
Heaven. Criticism has long ago demon-
strated the utter untenability of this view.
The *Zohar* made its first appearance in
Spain in the 13th century, and its contents show incontestably that not alone
must the work, as a whole, be considerably later than the 2nd century
(although many an idea and doctrine certainly does go as far back as that, and further
too), but that it could not possibly be the
production of a single author or a single
period of history. It is, like the *Yetsirah*
book, a syncretism. Many civilisations,
many faiths, and many philosophies went
to the making of it. All these were, in some
instances, taken in their original state and

incorporated in the work, while, in other instances, they found room in it only after they had passed through the crucible of the Jewish mind and had thus become ' judaised ' in the process. But that a goodly proportion of it is the development of many a doctrine embodied in the Talmud and Midrashim, there cannot be the least doubt. To ask whether this or that doctrine of Talmudic literature is indigenous to the Talmud or has its source elsewhere, is, of course, quite another matter. But that it reached the *Zohar* from the Talmud and Midrashim and their progeny, *directly*, is certain.

Where the foreign elements are drawn from is a fruitful subject of speculation amongst scholars. There is general admission, however, that Neoplatonism and Gnosticism are responsible for much.

And to this must be added a newer theory, which finds echoes of Persian Sūfism in the *Zohar*. The sūfi mystics were very numerous in Persia from the 8th century onwards, and it is maintained that the Jews of Persia, influenced by Sūfism, transmitted to the Jews of Spain (who were very numerous, very influential, and very distinguished in learning from the 10th to the 15th century) many mystical interpretations of esoteric tenets which in various shapes found an entrance into the *Zohar*.

Be this as it may, we must be on our guard

against following the mistaken opinion of a
certain set of Jewish theologians who would
have us regard the whole of the mediæval
Kabbalah (of which the *Zohar* is a conspicuous
and representative part) as a sudden and
strange importation from without. It is
really a continuation of the old stream of
Talmudic and Midrashic thought with the
admixture of extraneous elements picked up,
as was inevitable, by the stream's course
through many lands — elements the com-
mingling of which must have, in many ways,
transformed the original colour and nature of
the stream.

The *Zohar*, as was said above, purports to
be but a commentary on the Pentateuch.   It
is self-explanatory on this point. The following is a direct quotation :

" Woe unto the man," says Simeon ben
Yoḥai, " who sees in the Torah nought but
simple narratives and ordinary words. For
if, in truth, it contained only that, we should
have been able, even to-day, also to compose
a Torah which would be, in very much another
way, worthy of regard.   In order to find only
simple statements we should only have to
betake ourselves to the ordinary legislators,
among whom we could find valuable words
in even greater quantity. It would suffice
us to imitate them and to make a Law
after their words and example. But it is
not thus. Every word of the Torah con-

tains an elevated sense and a sublime mystery."

Here is a direct intimation of the *Zohar's* emphasis upon the existence of higher truths in the Bible. It continues :

" The narratives (or words) of the Law are the garment of the Law. Woe unto him who takes this garment for the Law itself ! It is in this sense that David spake, saying, ' Open thou mine eyes, that I may behold wondrous things out of thy Law ' (*Psalm,* cxix. 18). David wished to speak of that which is hidden beneath the garment of the Law. There are fools who, seeing a man covered with a beautiful garment, look no further than that ; and yet that which gives a worth to the garment is his body, and what is even more precious than that, his soul. The Law, too, has its body. There are precepts which one might call the body of the Law. The ordinary narratives which are intermingled are the garments with which the body is covered. Simpletons have regard only to the garments or narratives of the Law. . . . The better instructed pay no regard to the garment, but to the body which it encloses. Finally, the wise, the servants of the supreme King, they who inhabit the heights of Sinai, are concerned only with the soul which is the foundation of all else, which is the *real* Law. And in the time to come they will be prepared to gaze at the soul of that soul which breathes through the Law."

The mystical sense of the Law, then, is its highest and truest sense. What edifice of thought does the *Zohar* erect on this foundation ? It posits the cardinal principle that there is an esoteric as well as an exoteric reality in the phenomena of the world. The world is a series of emanations from the Divine. To quote the original :

" He is the beginning as well as the end of all stages (*dargin*) ; upon Him are stamped (*etrashim*) all the stages. But He can only be called *One*, in order to show that although He possesses many forms, He is nothing other than ONE " (i. fol. 21).

Or, to give a fuller and more striking version of the same thought :

" Before the Holy One (blessed be He) created this world, He went on creating worlds and destroying them. Whatsoever exists in this world, everything that has been in existence throughout all generations, *was in existence in His presence* (*kāmé*) in all their manifold forms " (iii. fol. 61).

In other words, the universe is the outward expression of the inner Divine thought. Everything germinated from the eternal archetypal Divine idea. Or as it is put in another way :

" He made this world of below to correspond with the world of above. Everything

which is above has its pattern here below
and *all constitutes a unity* " (ii. fol. 20).

What the *Zohar* thus aims at teaching us
is, that man, having the privilege to behold
everywhere the Divine image—the world
being an embodiment of God—can, if he will,
make his way to the Invisible Author of all ;
can have union with the Unseen. " Whatsoever belongs to the domain [literally ' side,'
sitrā] of the Spirit, thrusts itself forward and
is visible " (ii. fol. 20). The universe is
Divine Spirit materialised, and it is given to
man to have contact with it. The Rabbis
of the Talmud and Midrashim had an idea
of a sort of image of God which is immanent
in the universe. Thus, a passage in the
Tanḥuma (on *Genesis*, xxiii.) says : " If a
mortal king engraves his image upon a
tablet, the tablet is greater than the image.
But God is great, and yet His image is greater
than the whole world."

But it is only fair to add—and it bears out
the remark already made about the curious
mixture of ingredients which make up the
Zohar—that in conjunction with this high
note of thought there is another note which
strikes the modern reader as being of a piti-
fully inferior nature. The juxtaposition is de-
plorable. We are presented with an almost
unintelligible mass of mediæval astrology.
Thus : " In the firmament above which
covers all things, signs are engraven in which

are fixed hidden things and secrets. These
marks are those of the constellations and
the planets " (ii. fol. 74). Here is a tiny
quotation representative of a huge quantity of
the *Zohar's* material. " He who has to set
out on a journey in the morning must rise at
the break of day and must look towards the
east. He will behold letters moving in the
heavens, one ascending and another descending. These brilliant forms are those of
the letters with which God created the
heaven and the earth. They form His
mysterious and holy Name " (*Ibid.* 76).
This looks very much like a mixture of Pyth-
agorean theories of letters with mediæval
astrological notions. " When the spirits and
the souls come out of Eden [the *Zohar*, like
all the Kabbalah, abundantly teaches the
pre-existence of souls] they all possess a
certain appearance which, later on, is re-
flected in the face " (*Ibid.* 73). From this,
all sorts of the strangest facts of physiognomy
are seriously deduced.

In a work which professes to draw its
substance from the secret and esoteric aspect
of the Old Testament, and which, as we have
said, makes the seen world so much akin
to the unseen, it is only to be expected that
angelology should fill an important place.
The impetus to much of it is directly given
by a saying of the Talmud, to the effect that
" the righteous are greater than the minister-

ing angels " (*T.B. Sanhedrin*, 93a). This idea is just of a piece with the general drift of the *Zohar*. For, by its theories of emanation, and by its insistence on the idea of the macrocosm or of the world as being an evolution of the image of God and of man as a small copy of the world, a microcosm, it cannot but make man as the centre, the crown and consummation of all creation. Hence man must rank above the angels.

It is important to observe the framework of thought into which the *Zohar* fits its ideas on the relative positions of angels and men in the microcosm. The world as a manifestation of the Divine, as the material-ised expression of God's immanent activity, is really made up of four component parts (or 'worlds,' as the Kabbalah always styles them). These are : (*a*) the world of Azilut or emanation ; (*b*) the world of Beriah, *i.e.* creative ideas ; (*c*) the world of Yetsirah or creative formations ; (*d*) the world of 'Asiyah or creative matter.

The first term, Azilut, is based on the Hebrew verb *azal* in *Numbers*, xi. 17 (" And *I will take* of the spirit which is upon thee and will put it upon them "). The second, third, and fourth terms are derived from the three Hebrew verbs in *Isaiah*, xliii. 7, ' I have created,' ' I have formed,' ' I have made.' The world of Azilut constitutes the domain of the Ten Sefirot—which will be considered

in our next chapter. The world of Beriah
holds the Divine throne which emanates
from the light of the Sefirot, also the souls
of the pious. The world of Yetsirah is the
scene of the ' divine halls' (hekalot)—the
seven heavenly halls guarded by angels,
into which the ecstatic seekers for the
Merkabah (Chariot) strive to gain admission. The angels have their abode there,
presided over by Metatron ; and there also
are the souls of ordinary men (as distinguished from the pious). In the world of
'Asiyah are the lower order of angels—the
Ophanim, whose business it is to combat
evil and to receive the prayers of men. Thus,
seeing that the hierarchy of angels only
begins with the ' third world,' whereas the
souls of the pious belong to the ' second
world,' the position of man in the Divine
evolution is superior to that of the angel.

The idea of the active part thus played
by angels in the emanation-worlds of Jewish
mediæval mysticism is primarily derived
from such Old Testament verses as " he
maketh his angels winds [A.V. spirits] ;
his ministers a flaming fire " (Psalm, civ. 4),
which has already been quoted in a similar
connection before. But suppose we attempt
to rationalise the old-world allegorical language, what constructions would we place
upon these angelic activities in the scheme of
man and the universe ? Much light is shed

on the subject by the fact of the decisive names which are accorded to the angels— names which denote missions. Thus Raḥ- miel is the angel ot mercy, Tahariel is the angel of purity, Pedāel is the angel of de- liverance, Tsadkiel is the angel of justice, Raziel is the angel who guards the Divine secrets. Metatron is the master of all these, and it has been shown in a previous chapter how closely Metatron is allied to the Deity, playing in the world a *rôle* akin to that of the Deity. The inference from all these state- ments is that every particle of the natural world, every shred of man's organism, is saturated with some manifestation or other of the Divine Will—the Divine Will which is goodness and truth and love and justice made manifest and real. It is this impreg- nable Force underlying all phenomena that preserves the world in its course and that makes its manifold and variegated parts work in harmonious relations.

But what about the existence of sin and evil ? How can their existence be justified in a world such as the Zoharic mysticism implies—a world which is a series of emana- tions from the Divine, a world wherein God is eternally and intimately present in its every part, because the whole is but a mani- festation of Himself ? If all things, *i.e.* everything good and everything evil, are similarly and equally phases of the same

Divine Life, then the distinction between good and evil becomes meaningless. But to affirm this, is to deny the first principles of both religion and morality. It is the quagmire of pantheism. Does the *Zohar* lead to any pantheistic conclusion ? If not, how does it evade the difficulty ?

The reply to these queries is that the *Zohar* steers clear of the dangers of pantheism, and that it solves the problem of evil in a way which, while appearing highly unsatisfactory to the modern scientific Western mind, is quite in keeping with the intellectual level of the times in which its writers lived. Evil, sin, and their personifications, the demons, are termed *kĕlīfoth*, *i.e.* the coverings, wrappings, externals of all existing things. Just as the covering (or husk) of anything is not the real thing and far inferior to it, so sin and evil are, as it were, the gross, inferior, imperfect aspects of creation. And as the world is an emanation of the Divine, it follows that whatsoever in the world is evil, and not of the Divine, cannot be real. Hence evil is that which has no being; it is a sort of illusion; it is a state of absence, negation; it is a thing which merely appears to be but is not. It is symbolised, according to the *Zohar*, by the condition of the primæval chaos as described in *Genesis*, i. 2, *viz.* ' without form,' ' void,' ' darkness,' *i.e.* the absence of all visible form, order, life. By means of the creation of the world (which is an emanation of the Divine) the Infinite became, as it were, ' contracted ' (*Tsimtsum*) and took on certain attributes of the finite. To this finite belongs the ' darkness ' of the first chaos or, in other words, evil. Hence the finite stands at the uttermost extremity of the Divine emanation, *i.e.* the world. And as it is man's duty to strive after union with the Infinite, his pursuit of the finite leads him to that which lies at the extremity of the Divine nature rather than that which lies at the heart of it. This constitutes evil. It is a state of absence, a negation, because man who, like the universe, is but one of the manifestations of the Divine, can only attain the real when he seeks the Real who is his fount, his home.

It is of interest—and vital to an understanding of all Kabbalistic literature—to note some of the favourite technical terms employed, in addition to those already here mentioned in passing. A ubiquitous term is *En-Sof*, applied to the Deity. These words mean literally ' No End.' The Deity is boundless, endless. The *Zohar* was not the first mystical work to use the words. The underlying idea was probably supplied by the idea underlying the description of the Godhead in the philosophy of Ibn Gabirol, the Spanish-Hebrew poet and mystic philosopher

of the eleventh century. He describes the
Deity as the ' *shĕ-ĕn lo tiklah*,' *i.e.* the one
who has no bounds or ends. Ibn Gabirol
was a Neoplatonist, and much of his philosophy shows the influence upon him of
Plotinus. But he forsakes his master and
follows strictly in the line of Jewish tradition in one respect, *viz.* that in order, as he
thought, to safeguard the Jewish doctrine
of monotheism, the Deity must be freed from
the ascription to Him of all attributes.
Hence God can only be properly described
by a title which emphasises the negation
of all attributes. The *En-Sof* of the *Zohar*
and its predecessors is probably an echo of
this ultra-negative characterisation of the
Deity. Let us quote the *Zohar* :

" Before having created any shape in the
world, before having produced any form,
He was alone, without form, resembling
nothing. Who could comprehend Him as
He then was, before creation, since He had
no form ? It is forbidden to picture Him by
any form or under any shape whatsoever,
not even by His holy name, nor by a letter
[of the alphabet] nor by a point [the Yod,
which is the smallest letter in the Hebrew
alphabet, is usually designated as a point].
Such is the sense of the words, ' For ye saw
no manner of similitude on the day when the
Lord spake unto you in Horeb, out of the
midst of the fire' (*Deut.* iv. 15). This means

that you saw no other thing which you might possibly represent by a form or shape. But after He had created the form of the Heavenly Man (*Adam 'Ilā-ā*), He used him as a chariot (Merkābāh) on which to descend. He wished to be called by the form which consists of the holy name of Jahveh. He wished to make Himself known by His attributes, by each attribute separately. So He let Himself be styled as the God of pardon, the God of justice, the God omnipotent, the God of hosts and He who is (Jahveh). His object was to make thus intelligible what are His qualities and how His justice and His compassion extend over the world as well as over the works of men. For, had He not shed His brightness over all His creatures, how would we get to know Him ? How would it be true to say that the world is filled with His glory ? Woe unto the man who would dare to compare Him to even one of His own attributes ! Yet still less ought He to be likened unto the man who came from the earth and who is destined for death ! It is necessary to conceive of Him as above all creatures and all attributes. And then when these things have been removed, there is left neither attribute, nor shape, nor form " (ii. fol. 42).

From this characteristic extract, the following deductions are possible :

(*a*) God as the *En-Sof* and as a Being

utterly divested of attributes is an idea that
can only be postulated negatively. You
cannot tell what God is ; you can only tell
what He is not.   But if this be so, and if, as
is axiomatic to the *Zohar* and all the Kabbalah, the world is contained in God just
as a small vessel is contained in a larger,
and nothing exists outside of God, how can
creation be explained, whence and how
arose the universe ?   The universe is imperfect and finite, and its creation must have
involved, therefore, some change in the
character of God who *ex hypothesi* is perfect,
free from all attributes, and therefore free
from all possibility of change.   How could
this be ?   The answer is contained in the
Zohar's teaching on the Ten Sefirot, which
will be considered in our coming chapter.

(*b*) The idea of God using the Heavenly
Man (*Adam 'Ilā-ā*) as a chariot on which
to descend indicates a noteworthy identity
of teaching in the *Zohar* and Plotinus.
For both systems imply that there is a sort
of double movement in the universe, ' a
way down and a way up.'   There is a process
of Divine emanation, *i.e.* an outgoing of God,
a self-descent from His transcendent height
towards the lowly abodes of man.   And
correspondingly there is an ascent, a way up,
on the man's part.   For, just as to Plotinus,
the final stage of the soul's return journey
to its home in God, consists in its highest

experience (brought about by a withdrawal from desires and from objects of sense) of contact and union with God, so also, according to the *Zohar*, the three elements of which the soul is composed, *viz.* the rational (*neshāmāh*), the moral (*ruah*), and the vital (*nefesh*), are each of them, not only emanations from the Sefirot, but also have the potency of uniting him again with the Sefirot, and, in the case of the pious man, of uniting him with the highest of the Sefirot, the Crown or Supreme Intelligence.

(c) The idea of the Heavenly Man, or *Adam Kadmon* ('First' or 'Original' Man), or *Shechinta Tā-tā-ā* ('Lower' or 'Terrestrial' Shechinah), is vital to an understanding of the *Zohar* and of all Kabbalistic literature. It has resemblances to the Philonic exegesis on the distinction between "the heavenly man born in the image of God," and therefore having "no participation in any corruptible or earthlike essence," and "the earthly man," who was made " of loose material, called a lump of clay" (*On the Allegories of the Sacred Laws,* i. 12). One thinks also in this connection of Paul's views on the First Adam who was flesh and blood, a 'living soul,' and the Second Adam whom he describes as a 'quickening spirit' (1 *Cor.* xv. 45–49). There is, too, a Rabbinic *dictum* about a "spirit of Adam" which "moved upon the face of the waters" (as did the *Ruah* in *Genesis*, i. 2)—a pre-existent First Man.

The *Zohar* is possibly indebted for its treatment of the Heavenly Man to some one or, perhaps, all of these sources. It says as follows : " The Heavenly Man after he had manifested himself from out of the midst of the upper-world primitive obscurity, created the earthly man " (ii. 70 fol.). This means that the creation of man was the work, not of God, but of His supreme manifestation, His first emanation. This manifestation or emanation is the first of the Ten Sefirot (the Crown), which, as will be shown later, is the primal will of God which contained within itself the plan of the universe in its entire infinity of time and space. To say that the plan of the world in its entirety is contained in one of the emanations of God, is tantamount to saying that man (who is part of the world) is the product of an immanent Divine activity in the world. This immanent Divine activity is denoted by the term ' Heavenly Man,' as also by the term ' First of the Sefirot,' and, in varying senses, by all the Ten Sefirot.

But why, after all, such a title as ' Heavenly Man ' ? It is because, according to the *Zohar*, man is a copy of the universe below as well as of the universe above. Hence God in His creative capacity chose also the form of man. The *Zohar* puts it thus :

" Believe not that man consists solely of flesh, skin, bones, and veins. The real part of man is his soul, and the things just mentioned, the skin, flesh, bones, and veins, are only an outward covering, a veil, but are not the man. When man departs he divests himself of all the veils which cover him. And these different parts of our body correspond to the secrets of the Divine wisdom. The skin typifies the heavens which extend everywhere and cover everything like a garment. The flesh puts us in mind of the evil side of the universe. The bones and the veins symbolise the Divine chariot, the inner powers of man which are the servants of God. But they are all but an outer covering. For, inside man, there is the secret of the *Heavenly Man*. . . . Everything below takes place in the same manner as everything above. This is the meaning of the remark that God created man in His own image. But just as in the heavens, which cover the whole universe, we behold different shapes brought about by the stars and the planets to teach us concerning hidden things and deep secrets, so upon the skin which covers our body there are shapes and forms which are like planets and stars to our bodies. All these shapes have a hidden meaning, and are observed by the sages who are able to read the face of man " (ii. 76a).

CHAPTER VII

THE TEN SEFIROT

ALL finite creatures are, in divergent senses and varying degrees, part and parcel of the Deity. *Creatio ex nihilo* is unthinkable, seeing that God, in the Neoplatonic view, is the Perfect One, ' an undivided One,' to whom no qualities or characteristics can be ascribed, and to whom, therefore, no such idea as that of intention or purpose, or change or movement, can be applied. All existences are emanations from the Deity. The Deity reveals Himself in all existences because He is immanent in them. But though dwelling in them, He is greater than they. He is apart from them. He transcends them.

The foregoing might be said to be a general *résumé* of the philosophy of the Ten Sefirot. To quote a passage from the section of the *Zohar* called the *Idra Zūtta* ('Small Assembly'):

" The Most Ancient One [1] is at the same

---

[1] One of the favourite names for God in the mediæval Kabbalah. It is based on the phrase in *Daniel*, vii. 9, 13, 22, ' ancient of days.'

time the most Hidden of the hidden. He is separated from all things, and is at the same time not separated from all things. For all things are united in Him, and He unites Himself with all things. There is nothing which is not in Him. He has a shape, and one can say that He has not one. In assuming a shape, He has given existence to all things. He made ten lights spring forth from His midst, lights which shine with the form which they have borrowed from Him, and which shed everywhere the light of a brilliant day. The Ancient One, the most Hidden of the hidden, is a high beacon, and we know Him only by His lights, which illuminate our eyes so abundantly. His Holy Name is no other thing than these lights."

The ' ten lights ' are, of course, the Ten Sefirot, the ten successive emanations from the Godhead, the ten powers or qualities which were latent from all eternity in the Godhead. But what is meant by saying that ' His Holy Name is no other thing but these lights ' ? We turn to another passage in the *Zohar* for the explanation. It reads as follows :

" The name ' I am ' [in Hebrew, *ĕhĕyĕh* ; see *Exodus*, iii. 14, ' I am that I am '—in Hebrew, *ĕhĕyĕh ăshĕr ĕhĕyĕh*] signifies the unity of all things. Afterwards He brought out that light which is the celestial mother, and when she bare a child, then He called Himself ' that I am ' (*ăshĕr ĕhĕyĕh*). And

when all else came into existence, and everything became perfected and in its right place,
then He called Himself Jahveh " (iii. 65).

The passage seems hopeless as regards a
meaning. But on deeper consideration it
becomes quite clear. The Divine Name, ' I
am that I am,' is inferior to the Divine Name
Jahveh. It typifies an earlier, less-devel-
oped stage. The student of Hebrew will
readily know why this is. Although translated into English as ' I am that I am ' it
belongs grammatically to what the Semitic
philologists call the ' imperfect tense,' repre-
senting an unfinished action. But ' Jahveh '
is grammatically the ' present tense ' (*i.e.*
a noun formed from this tense). Hence ' I
am that I am ' signifies the Godhead as He
was when He existed as the ' Hidden of the
hidden,' *i.e.* when He was the ' undivided
One,' the Absolute containing in Himself the
All, before He had, so to speak, unfolded
Himself in His creative acts, before any
emanations had radiated out from Him.
But ' Jahveh ' denotes the crown and summit
of the Divine self-manifestation ; in other
words, it denotes God as immanent in all the
numberless parts of the cosmos, which is but
a revelation, an embodiment of the Divine
thought. The idea of the ' celestial mother '
having a child is part of the *Zohar's* doctrine
of emanation, where, as will be shown later
on, a certain one of the Ten Sefirot is

called 'father' (*Abba*) and another is called
'mother' (*Imma*), and from the union of the
two, there is born another of the Sefirot,
called the 'son' (*Ben*).

Hence to say that 'God's Holy Name is
no other thing than these lights' is but to
say that the Sefirot which represent the
world as the copy of an ever-active, ever-
energising God, sum up all that the Divine
Name stands for. And that the Divine
Name denotes a strongly mystical aspect of
the relation between God and the universe
is abundantly clear from the Essenic literature, as well as from the Book *Yetsirah*.
In fact, it appears occasionally in this sense,
in the Talmudic and Midrashic records (see,
e.g., T.B. Pesaḥim, 55b), and the germ of the
idea can be traced back to the Old Testament,
to such phrases as: "This is my name for
ever, and this is my memorial unto all
generations" (*Exodus*, iii. 15); or: "Thy
name, O Lord, endureth for ever; and thy
memorial, O Lord, throughout all generations" (*Psalm*, cxxxv. 13).

One of the clearest passages in the *Zohar*
stating what the Ten Sefirot are, is the
following :

"For the waters of the sea are limitless
and shapeless. But when they are spread
over the earth, then they produce a shape
(*dimiōn*), and we can calculate like this : The
source of the waters of the sea and the force

which it emits to spread itself over the soil,
are two things. Then an immense basin is
formed by the waters just as is formed when
one makes a very deep digging. This basin
is filled by the waters which emanate from
the source; it is the sea itself, and can be
regarded as a third thing. This very large
hollow [of waters] is split up into seven canals,
which are like so many long tubes, by means
of which the waters are conveyed. The
source, the current, the sea, and the seven
canals form together the number *ten*. And
should the workman who constructed these
tubes come to break them up, then the waters
return to their source, and there remains
naught but the *débris* and the water dried up.
It is thus that the *Cause of causes* has created
the Ten Sefirot. The *Crown* is the source
whence there springs a light without end,
from which comes the name *En-Sof*, *i.e.*
Infinite, designating the *Supreme Cause*; for
while in this state it possesses neither shape
nor figure; there are no means of compre-
hending it; there is no way of knowing it.
It is in this sense that it has been said, ' Seek
not the things that are too hard for thee '
(*Ecclesiasticus*, iii. 21). Then there is formed
a vessel contracted to a mere point [the letter
Yod, the smallest letter in the Hebrew
alphabet] into which the Divine light pene-
trates. It is the source of *Wisdom*, it is
Wisdom itself, in virtue of which the *Supreme*

Cause is called the God of Wisdom. Afterwards, it [*i.e.* the *Supreme Cause*] constructs a channel, wide as the sea, which is called *Intellect* [or *Intelligence*]. From this, comes the title of ' God who understands ' [*i.e.* is intelligent]. We must know, however, that God only understands and is wise by means of His own essential substance ; for Wisdom does not merit the title by itself, but only by the instrumentality of Him who is wise and who has produced it from the light which emanates from Him. One cannot conceive what ' knowing ' is by itself, but by Him who is the ' knowing One,' and who fills it with His own essential substance.

" Finally, the sea is divided into seven parts, and there result [from this division] the seven precious channels which are called : (*a*) Compassion (or Greatness), (*b*) Justice (or Force), (*c*) Beauty, (*d*) Victory, (*e*) Glory, (*f*) Royalty, and (*g*) Foundation.[1] It is for this reason that God is called the ' Great ' or the ' Compassionate,' the ' Strong,' the ' Magnificent,' the ' God of Victories,' the ' Creator to whom all glory belongs,' and the ' Foundation of all things.' It is this latter attribute which sustains all the others, as well as the totality of the worlds. And yet, He is also the King of the universe, for all things are in His power whether He wills to lessen the number of the channels and increase the

[1] Some authorities invert the order of *f* and *g*.

light which springs from them, or whether He wills the contrary " (foll. 42, 43).

According to this characteristic passage, the Sefirot are the Names of the Deity—but only in the deeply mystical sense of ' Names ' as has been referred to above. The Divine Name is, on this understanding, equivalent to the Presence of God, the eternal Source of the power and intelligence enshrined in the constitution of the world and the heart of man. The Ten Sefirot together are thus a picture of how an infinite, undivided, unknowable God takes on the attributes of the finite, the divided, the knowable, and thus becomes the cause of, the power lying at the bottom of, all the multifarious modes of existence in the finite plane—all of which are thus a reflection of the Divine. The Sefirot have no real tangible existence at all. They are but a figure of speech showing the Divine immanence in all cosmic phenomena, in all the grades of man's spiritual and moral achievement.

It should, however, be pointed out here, that the functions and natures of the Sefirot are described by the *Zohar* in the most enigmatic of enigmatic language. Hence different deductions have always been possible, and hence, too, the rise of more than one school of *Zohar* interpretation. . The view mostly followed—and it may be said to be the universally-accepted standard—is

that of the school of Luria and Cordovero,
the two most famous Kabbalists of the six-
teenth century.

Let us now consider each of the Sefirot
separately. What we shall say will amount
in substance, though not in form, to a commentary on the lengthy passage from the
Zohar previously quoted. Prior to the first
of the Sefirot must come, what our extract
has termed the *Supreme Cause* (literally the
' Cause of causes ') or the *En-Sof*. What is
the relation of the *En-Sof* to the Sefirot ?
According to the theories of Luria and
Cordovero, all the Sefirot emanate from the
En-Sof, who, although eternally present in
them all, is not comprehended in them, but
transcends them. All modes of existence and
thought embody some fragment of the *En-Sof*,
but, with all this, the *En-Sof* is divided from
them by an impassable gulf. He remains
the hidden, unapproachable Being. This is
why, while each of the Sefirot has a well-
known name, the *En-Sof* has no name. Just
as in the Talmudic mysticism of the Shechinah
the idea of a universally-diffused, all-penetrating Deity is conveyed by the metaphor
of light, so in the case of the mediæval
Kabbalah the *En-Sof* is likewise spoken of
as Light (*Or En-Sof*=' The Infinite Light ').
The Christian mystics also favoured the same
figure. Closely connected with this teaching
is the general Kabbalistic doctrine of *Tsim-*

tsūm, i.e. contraction. It, too, is found in the Talmud and Midrashim, and it is from them that the Kabbalah, most likely, received it. Thus *Genesis Rabba,* iv. 5, dwells on the paradox (mentioned also by Philo) of the world being too small to hold God, but yet the space between the Ark's staves being large enough. The Kabbalistic idea of *Tsimtsūm* is an attempt to explain the contraction or limitation of the *En-Sof* (the Infinite), in order to make possible the emanation of the Sefirot, *i.e.* in order to produce the finite world of phenomena. The universal infiltration of the light of the *En-Sof,* its diffusion throughout all the Sefirot, gave rise to the idea of the existence of a changeable and an unchangeable element in each of the Sefirot. The former represents the material, outward, perishable side of man and the universe. The latter is the changeless, unfading eternal quality embedded in man and the universe. It is just this dual aspect which is referred to in the long extract from the *Zohar* quoted above, in the words : " Should the workman who constructed these tubes come to break them up, then the waters return to their source, and there remains naught but the *débris* and the water dried up." In other words, should the *En-Sof* withdraw its eternal immanent light and life from any one of the Sefirot, or, to speak in untechnical language, should God, who is the Life of the universe, the Power lying beneath and behind all phenomena, by some miraculous intervention withdraw or suspend some fragment of Himself, then the cosmos reverts to chaos.

The first of the Ten Sefirot is the Crown (in Hebrew, *Keter*). It is of importance for the reader to note that whereas Neo-platonism is largely responsible for the basis of the *Zohar's* doctrines of emanation, the names of the Sefirot and the teaching embraced and conveyed by those names are entirely drawn from the field of the Old Testament and Rabbinical theology. All ages of Jewish thought (as well as of Jewish art) employ the word, image, and idea of a ' crown ' in a considerable variety of senses. In Biblical Hebrew there are no less than five different words all indiscriminately translated as ' crown,' but denoting really either different forms of the thing or different prominent portions of it. In the Apocryphal and Rabbinical literature men ' crowned ' themselves in all sorts of ways, and the crown was symbolic of a host of religious ideas. In the theological realm, ' crown ' played many parts.

Only two references—both germane to our subject—can be quoted here. In *T.B. Berachoth,* 17a, it is said : " In the world to come there is neither eating nor drinking, nor marrying, nor bargaining, nor envy, nor hatred, nor quarrel ; but the righteous sit, *with crowns upon their heads,* and feed upon the splendour of the Shechinah, as it is said of the nobles of the children of Israel, ' He laid not His hand upon them, but they saw God, and this was equivalent to their eating and their drinking ' [so the Targumic paraphrase of *Exodus,* xxiv. 11]." ***T.B.*** *Megillah,* 15b, says : " In the time to come, God will be a *crown of glory* upon the head of each saint, as it is written, ' In that day shall the Lord of Hosts be for a crown of glory, and for a diadem of beauty, unto the residue of His people ' (*Isaiah,* xxviii. 5)." Hence, it is not hard to discover by what process of reasoning the mediæval Jewish mystics thought it fitting to designate the first of the Sefirot as the Crown.

" It is," says the *Zohar,* " the principle of all principles, the hidden Wisdom, the Crown which the Highest of the high, and by which all crowns and diadems are crowned " (iii. 288). It is the first of the emanations from the *En-Sof.* The latter being, as has been said above, the infinite, hidden, unknowable Being, the Crown represents, as it were, the first stage by which the Infinite Being takes on the properties of the finite and becomes drawn out of His impenetrable isolation. But, nevertheless, the Crown is an absolute indivisible unity, possessing no attributes or qualities, and baffling all

analysis and description. It is, to quote
the original, a ' *nekūdah peshtūah,*' *i.e.* ' a
simple point,' or '*nekūda rishōnah,*' *i.e.* ' a
primordial point.' The idea here is that
the first manifestation of the Divine is a
point, *i.e.* a unity, unanalysable, indescribable, and yet possessing the All. In other
words, it is the Hegelian idea of ' pure being '
(*das reine sein*). This ' pure being ' or
' existence ' is the thought or reason of
God. The starting-point of everything is
the thought as it existed in God. The universe is this ' thought ' of God. It is in
this ' thought ' of God that everything was
originally embraced. The first of the Sefirot
denotes, then, the primordial Divine Thought
(or Divine Will, as the Hebrew commentators
often style it) ; and to say this is tantamount
to saying that the Crown contained within
itself the plan of the universe in its infinity of
time and space, in its endless varieties of form,
colour, and movement. And it is an emanation from the *En-Sof* who, while immanent
in the Crown, and hence immanent in all the
Sefirot, yet transcends them all.

The Crown, for the reasons just mentioned, is ofttimes styled *Resha Hivra, i.e.*
the ' White Head '—' head ' denoting the
idea of source, and ' white ' being the blend
of all the colours (just as the Crown is the
blend of all forms in the cosmos). But the
idea may possibly be drawn from *Daniel,*

vii. 9, where " One that was ancient of days
did sit ; his raiment was white as snow, and
the hair of his head like pure wool " (cf.
1 *Enoch*, xiv. 18–22 ; *Revelation*, i. 14). The
original Aramaic for ' ancient of days ' is
' *attik* ' ; and this, too, is a name for the first
of the Sefirot, and is frequently employed in
the Kabbalah, generally as a designation of
the Deity.

Wisdom and Intelligence are the second
and third of the Ten Sefirot. They are
parallel emanations from the Crown or first
Sefirah. Here we alight upon an interesting
feature of this mysticism, *viz.* the application of the idea of the sexual relationship
to the solution of the problem of existence.
" When the Ancient One, the Holy One,
desired to bring all things into being, He
created them all as male and female "
(iii. 290). Wisdom is the ' father,' *i.e.* the
masculine active principle which engenders
all things and imposes on them form and
measure (an idea derived from *Job*, xxviii.
12). Intelligence is the ' mother,' the
passive, receptive principle (derived from
Proverbs, ii. 3, " Yea, if thou cry after discernment," *i.e.* ' Binah ' in Hebrew ; and the
word rendered by ' if ' can, by the slightest
alteration of a vowel, be rendered by
' mother,' and thus the passage is translated
by the *Zohar* as, " Yea, if mother thou
callest discernment "). Out of the union of

Wisdom and Intelligence comes a 'son' who is dowered with the characteristics of both parents. This son is Reason (*Da'at*), which is, by the way, not regarded as an independent Sefirah. These three, father, mother, son (*i.e.* the two Sefirot, viz. Wisdom and Intelligence, and their offspring Reason), hold and unite in themselves all that which has been, which is, and which will be. But they in their turn are all united to the first Sefirah (the Crown), who is the all-comprehensive One who is, was, and will be.

Here one meets again with a foreshadowing of the Hegelian teaching concerning the identity of thought and being. The universe is an expression of the ideas or the absolute forms of intelligence. Cordovero says :

" The first three Sefirot must be considered as one and the same thing. The first represents 'knowledge,' the second 'the knower,' the third 'that which is known.' The Creator is Himself, at one and the same time, knowledge, the knower, and the known. Indeed, His manner of knowing does not consist in applying His thought to things outside Him ; it is by self-knowledge that He knows and perceives everything which is. There exists nothing which is not united to Him and which He does not find in His own essence. He is the type of all being, and all things exist in Him under their most pure and most perfect form. . . . It is thus that all existing things in the universe have their form in the Sefirot, and the Sefirot have theirs in the source from which they emanate."

Thus, the first three Sefirot form a triad constituting the world as a manifestation of the Divine Thought. The remaining seven Sefirot likewise fall into triads. The Divine Thought is the source whence emanate two opposing principles, one active or masculine, the other passive or feminine. The former is Mercy (*Ḥesed*), the latter is Justice (*Dīn*). From the union of these two there results Beauty (*Tifĕrĕth*). The logical connections between these three principles, as they stand in the *Zohar*, are extremely difficult to fathom. But Cordovero and other Hebrew commentators give us the needed solution of the problem. The Sefirot Mercy and Justice represent the universe as being at one and the same time an expansion and contraction of the Divine Will. Mercy, as the active masculine principle, is the life-giving, ever-productive because ever-forgiving power innate in man and the universe. Justice is the necessarily-opposed immanent faculty holding in check what would otherwise prove to be the excesses of Mercy. The theology of the Talmudic Rabbis shows itself unmistakably here. In the beginning, say the Rabbis, God thought to create the universe by the 'attribute of justice' (designated by the word 'Jahveh'). But on considering that the universe could not exist by ' justice ' alone, He determined to join the ' attribute of mercy ' (designated by the word ' Elohim ') with the ' attribute of justice,' and to create the universe—as He finally did—by the dual means. Likewise in the *Zohar* mysticism, the moral order of the universe can only follow on a combination of the Sefirot Mercy and Justice. And the inevitable product of the union is the sixth Sefirah, Beauty. The reasoning is apparent. We have thus far seen how the first triad of Sefirot pictures God as the immanent thinking power of the universe, and how the second triad interprets God as the immanent moral power of the universe.

The third triad are : Victory (*Nezaḥ*), Glory (*Hōd*), and Foundation (*Yesōd*). The first of these is the masculine active principle. The second is the feminine passive principle, while the third is the effect of their combination. What aspect of a God-saturated world do these three Sefirot point to ? The *Zohar* tells us, as follows : " Extension, variety [or multiplication], and force are gathered together in them ; and all forces that come out, come out from them, and it is for this reason that they are called Hosts [*i.e.* armies or forces]. They are [the two fore-mentioned Sefirot] Victory and Glory " (iii. 296). The allusion is obviously to the physical, dynamic aspect of the universe, the ceaseless, developing world with its multiplicity and variety of forces, changes and movements. From their coalescence comes the ninth Sefirah, Foundation. Rightly so; for it is the endless, changeless ebb and flow of the world's forces that, in the last resort, guarantees the stability of the world and builds up its ' foundation.' It creates the reproductive power of nature, endows it with, as it were, a generative organ from which all things proceed, and upon which all things finally depend.

The last of the Sefirot is Royalty (*Malkūt*). Its function is not very apparent, and its existence may be due to the desire on the part of the Kabbalists to make up the number ten—a number which looms largely in the Old Testament literature, as well as in the theology of the Talmud, Midrashim, and Philo. Generally speaking, this tenth Sefirah indicates the abiding truth of the harmonious co-operation of all the Sefirot, thus making the universe in its orderliness and in its symmetry a true and exact manifestation of the Divine Mind—an *'Olam Azilut, i.e.* a world of emanation, as the Kabbalists themselves style it.

The fact that the Sefirot fall into triads or trinities, and the ascription to them of such sexual titles as ' father,' ' mother,' ' son,' has encouraged many an apologist for Christianity to say that the essential Christian dogma of the Trinity is implicit in the Jewish mystical literature. But it is beyond a doubt that the resemblance is quite a matter of accident. It cannot be too often repeated that there is a substantial admixture of foreign elements in all branches of the Kabbalah. The philosophy of Salomon Ibn Gabirol (which largely echoes Plato), Neoplatonism, Gnosticism, Philonism, and other systems have all left indelible traces. But Christianity, be it remembered, besides being a debtor to Judaism, is a debtor to these sources as well ; so that what appears to be Christian may be, in reality, Jewish ; a development of the original material by an unbroken succession of Jewish minds. This original material is the old Talmudic and Midrashic exegesis upon which was foisted the alien philosophies just alluded to. That there should be a resultant resemblance to Christianity is quite a normal outcome ; but it is beyond dispute that the Christian Trinity and the trinities of the Ten Sefirot lie in quite distinct planes.

The Jewish Prayer Book echoes much of the theological sentiment of the *Zohar*. There is a fine hymn in the Sabbath-morning service which, while giving a noteworthy prominence to the *names* of the Sefirot, reproduces with a charming simplicity of Hebrew diction, the main body of the Zoharic doctrine, its cosmology, angelology, astrology, and psychology. It is as follows : [1] " God,

[1] From the Authorised Daily Prayer Book, ed. Singer, p. 129.

the Lord over all works, blessed is He, and
ever to be blessed by the mouth of everything that hath breath. His greatness and
goodness fill the world ; *knowledge* (*Da'at*)
and *understanding* (*Tebūnah* = *Bīnah*) [*i.e. intelligence*] surround Him. He is exalted above
the holy Ḥayot, and is adorned in *glory* (*Kabod*
= *Hōd*) above the celestial chariot (*merkabah*) ;
purity and rectitude are before his throne,
loving-kindness (*Ḥesed*) and tender mercy
before his *glory*. The luminaries are good
which our God hath created : He formed
them with *knowledge*, understanding, and discernment ; He gave them might and power
to rule in the midst of the world. They are
full of lustre,[1] and they radiate brightness ;
beautiful is their lustre throughout all the
world. They rejoice in their going forth, and
are glad in their returning ; they perform
with awe the will of their Master. *Glory*
and *honour* they render unto his name,
exultation and rejoicing at the remembrance
of his *sovereignty* (*Malkūt*). He called unto
the sun, and it shone forth in light ; He looked
and ordained the figure of the moon. All the
hosts on high render praise unto Him, the
Seraphim, the Ophanim, and the holy Ḥayot
ascribing *glory* (lit. beauty, *i.e. Tifĕrĕth*) and
greatness."[2]

---

[1] *Ziv* in Hebrew, a mystical term for the shining of the
Shechinah.
[2] Another appellation for *Ḥesed*, the fourth Sefirah.

CHAPTER VIII

THE SOUL

As in all systems of mysticism, the soul plays a towering part in the theology of the *Zohar*. Mysticism's centre of gravity is the close kinship between the human and the Divine; and the only avenue through which this kinship can become real to us is the soul. The soul, as a spiritual entity playing the highest of high parts in man's relation with the Unseen, is not a conspicuous element of either the Old Testament or the Talmudic-Midrashic writings; and the critics of Judaism have a way of saying harsh things about that religion on the grounds of its deficiency in this respect. But the shortcoming is amply atoned for by the large part assigned to the function of the soul in all branches of the mediæval Kabbalah.

That the *Zohar* is a debtor to a double source—the Talmudic teachings and the teachings of the Neoplatonists — is very apparent from its treatment of the soul. A passage from the former reads as follows: "Just as the soul fills the body, so God

fills the world. Just as the soul bears the
body, so God endures the world. Just as the
soul sees but is not seen, so God sees but is
not seen. Just as the soul feeds the body
[*i.e.* spiritually, intellectually], so God gives
food to the world " (*T.B. Berachoth*, 10a).
The predominant influence of the soul over
the body, the body as overflown in all its
parts by the soul and dependent upon it
for the source of its life—these are the implications of the passage just quoted ; and
they are the substratum of the Zoharic ideas
of the soul.

Neoplatonism gave to the *Zohar* the
idea of the soul as an emanation from the
' Overmind ' of the universe. There was
originally one ' Universal Soul,' or ' Oversoul,' which, as it were, broke itself up
and encased itself in individual bodies. All
individual souls are, hence, fragments of the
' Oversoul,' so that although they are distinct from one another they are, in reality,
all *one*. Thus, to quote the *Zohar* :

" At the time when God desired to create
the universe, it came up in His will before
Him, and He formed all the souls which
were destined to be allotted to the children
of men. The souls were all before Him in
the forms which they were afterwards
destined to bear inside the human body.
God looked at each one of them, and He
saw that many of them would act corruptly

in the world. When the time of each
arrived, it was summoned before God, who
said to it : ' Go to such and such a part of
the universe, enclose thyself in such and
such a body.' But the soul replied : ' O
sovereign of the universe, I am happy in
my present world, and I desire not to leave
it for some other place where I shall be
enslaved and become soiled.' Then the
Holy One (blessed be He) replied : ' From
the day of thy creation thou hast had no
other destiny than to go into the universe
whither I send thee.' The soul, seeing
that it must obey, sorrowfully took the way
to earth and came down to dwell in our
midst " (ii. 96).

There is more than one echo of Plotinus—
the master-mind of Neoplatonism—in this
Zoharic extract. ' The world coming up in
His will before Him ' is Plotinus' teaching
about God thinking out the original patterns
of all things, the first manifestation of God
being Thought. ' The souls were all before
Him in the forms which they were afterwards destined to bear ' is clearly an allusion
to the splitting-up of the Oversoul, so that its
fragments might get embodied in individuals
—as Plotinus taught. But although the
Zohar, like Plotinus, draws a distinction
between *lower* souls (' they who would act
corruptly in the world ') and higher souls,
it, unlike Plotinus, makes every soul de-

scend into some body. Plotinus has quite
a different teaching.

" The lower soul desires a body and lives
in the stage of sense. . . . The higher soul,
on the other hand, transcends the body,
' rides upon it,' as the fish is in the sea or
as the plant is in the air. This higher soul
never absolutely leaves its home, its *being*
is not here but ' yonder,' or, in the language
of Plotinus, ' The soul always leaves something of itself above ' " (Rufus M. Jones,
Studies in Mystical Religion, p. 74).

According to the *Zohar*, while there are
distinctions there, too, between superior
and inferior souls—as is shown by their
belonging to a higher or lower Sefirah—
they must all descend to earth and unite
with the body, returning, all of them, at
death to their fountain-head, God.

The *Zohar* is, after all, but a commentary
on the Hebrew Bible, and however much it
may, at times, forsake the traditional Jewish
pathways in favour of alien philosophies,
it is always strictly conservative where the
fundamental axioms of the Jewish faith are
concerned. That every body possesses a
soul which in its pristine form is ' pure,'
that recompense in an after-life awaits it on
a scale commensurate with its deserts, is an
impregnable tenet of Judaism. The *Zohar*,
wherever it may wander, must come back
to this central point.

The soul is a trinity. It comprises three elements, *viz.* : (*a*) *Neshāmāh*, the rational element which is the highest phase of existence; (*b*) *Ruaḥ*, the moral element, the seat of good and evil, the ethical qualities; (*c*) *Nefesh*, the gross side of spirit, the vital element which is *en rapport* with the body, and the mainspring of all the movements, instincts, and cravings of the physical life.

There is a strong reflection of Platonic psychology in these three divisions or powers of the soul. More than one mediæval Jewish theologian was a Platonist, and in all probability the *Zohar* is a debtor to these. The three divisions of the soul are emanations from the Sefirot. The *Neshāmāh*, which, as has been said, is the soul in its most elevated and sublimest sense, emanates from the Sefirah of Wisdom. The *Ruaḥ*, which denotes the soul in its ethical aspect, emanates from the Sefirah of Beauty. The *Nefesh*, which is the animal side of the soul, is an emanation from the Sefirah of Foundation, that element of divinity which comes, most of all, into contact with the material forces of earth.

To sum up the matter in general and untechnical language, the three divisions or aspects of the human soul enable man to fit himself into the plan and framework of the cosmos, give him the power to do his

multifarious duties towards the multifarious
portions of the world,—the world which is
a manifestation of God's thought, a copy of
the celestial universe, an emanation of the
Divine.   The *Zohar* puts it poetically thus :

" In these three [*i.e. Neshāmāh, Ruaḥ,
Nefesh*] we find an exact image (*diyūkna*)
of what is above in the celestial world.   For
all three form only *one* soul, one being, where
all is *one*.   The *Nefesh* [*i.e.* the lowest side
of soul] does not in itself possess any light.
This is why it is so tightly joined to the body,
acquiring for it the pleasures and the foods
which it needs.   It is of it that the sage says,
' She giveth meat to her household and their
task to her maidens ' (*Proverbs*, xxxi. 15).
' Her household ' means the body which is
fed.   ' Her maidens ' are the limbs which
obey the dictates of the body.   Above the
Nefesh is the *Ruaḥ* [the ethical soul] which
dominates the *Nefesh*, imposes laws upon
it and enlightens it as much as its nature
requires.   And then high above the *Ruaḥ*
is the *Neshāmāh*, which in its turn rules the
Ruaḥ and sheds upon it the light of life.
The *Ruaḥ* is lit up by this light, and depends
entirely upon it.   After death, the *Ruaḥ*
has no rest.   The gates of Paradise (*Eden*)
are not opened to it until the time when
Neshāmāh has reascended to its source,
to the Ancient of the ancients, in order to
become filled with Him throughout eternity.

For the *Neshāmāh* is always climbing back again towards its source " (ii. 142).

It can be gathered from this passage, as from many similar ones which might have been usefully quoted had space allowed, that *Neshāmāh* is only realised, that man only becomes conscious of *Neshāmāh*, after death. A whole lifetime is necessary (and in some cases *more* than one lifetime, as we shall see) in order that *Neshāmāh* should be able to mount up again to the Infinite source from which it emanated. And it is the inevitable destiny of *Neshāmāh* to climb back and become one with the 'Ancient of ancients.'

But if *Neshāmāh* is so exalted, so sacrosanct, why should it have emanated from its immaculate source at all, to become tainted with earth ? The *Zohar* anticipates our question and gives its answer as follows :

" If thou inquirest why it [*i.e.* the soul] cometh down into the world from so exalted a place and putteth itself at such a distance from its source, I reply thus : It may be likened to an earthly monarch to whom a son is born. The monarch takes the son to the countryside, there to be nourished and trained until such a time as he is old enough to accustom himself to the palace of his father. When the father is told that the education of his son is completed, what does he do out of his love for him ? In order

to celebrate his home-coming, he sends for
the queen, the mother of the lad.   He brings
her into the palace and rejoices with her the
whole day long.

"It is thus with the Holy One (blessed be
He).   He, too, has a son by the queen.   This
son is the high and holy soul.   He conducts
it to the countryside, *i.e.* to the world, in order
to grow up there and gain an acquaintance
with the customs appertaining to the royal
palace.   When the Divine King perceives
that the soul has completed its growth, and
the time is ripe for recalling it to Himself,
what does He do out of His love for it ?   He
sends for the queen, brings her into the
palace, and brings the soul in too.   The soul,
forsooth, does not bid adieu to its earthly
tenement before the queen has come to
unite herself with it, and to lead it into the
royal apartment where it is to live for ever.

"And the people of the world are wont
to weep when the son [*i.e.* the soul] takes its
leave of them.   But if there be a wise man
amongst them, he says to them, Why weep
ye ?   Is he not the son of the King ?   Is it
not meet that he should take leave of you
to live in the palace of his father ?   It
was for this reason that Moses, who knew
the Truth, on seeing the inhabitants of
earth mourning for the dead, exclaimed,
' Ye are the children of the Lord your God ;
ye shall not cut yourselves, nor make any

baldness between your eyes for the dead'
(*Deut.* xiv. 1). If all good men knew this,
they would hail with delight the day when it
behoves them to bid adieu to the world.
Is it not the height of glory for them when
the queen [*i.e.* the Shechinah, the Divine
Presence] comes down into the midst of
them to lead them into the palace of the
king to enjoy the delights thereof for ever-
more ? " (i. 245).

It should be noted, by the way, that there
are many instances in Talmudic literature,
of men seeing the Shechinah at the hour of
death. It is the signal of the return of
Neshāmāh to its home, the Oversoul, of
which it is but a loosened fragment ; and
the return can only begin after it has completed its education within the life-limits of
an earthly body.

It seems to follow, as a necessary corollary
from the foregoing doctrine, that the *Zohar*
must give countenance to some theory of the
transmigration of souls. If it is imperative
upon *Neshāmāh* to climb back again to the
Oversoul and obtain union with it ; and if,
in order to effect this end, it must previously
have reached the summit of purity and perfection, then it stands to reason that its
sojourn within the confines of one body
may, on occasions, be inadequate to enable it
to reach this high and exacting condition.
Hence it must ' experience ' other bodies,

and it must repeat the ' experience ' until
such a time as it shall have elevated and
refined itself to the pitch at which it will be
able to become one again with the fountain
from which it emanated. The *Zohar* does
contain some such tenet as this, although for
the full and systematic treatment of the subject one has to look to the Kabbalistic writers
who built upon the *Zohar*. The *Zohar* states
as follows :

" All souls must undergo transmigration ;
and men do not understand the ways of the
Holy One (blessed be He). They know not
that they are brought before the tribunal
both before they enter into this world and
after they leave it. They know not the many
transmigrations and hidden trials which they
have to undergo, nor do they know the number of souls and spirits (*Ruaḥ* and *Nefesh*)
which enter into the world, and which do not
return to the Palace of the Heavenly King.
Men do not know how the souls revolve like
a stone which is thrown from a sling. But
the time is drawing nigh when these hidden
things will be revealed " (ii. 99).

To the minds of the Kabbalists, transmigration is a necessity not alone on the
grounds of their particular theology—the
soul must reach the highest stage of its
evolution before it can be received again into
its eternal home—but on moral grounds as
well. It is a vindication of Divine justice to

mankind. It settles the harassing query which all ages have propounded : Why does God permit the wicked to flourish as the green bay tree, whereas the righteous man is allowed to reap nothing but sorrow and failure ? And the only way for reconciling the dismal fact of child-suffering with the belief in a good God, is by saying that the pain is a retribution to the soul for sin committed in some one or more of its previous states. As has been already mentioned, the Jewish literature of this subject of transmigration is an exceedingly rich one. But it lies outside the scope of the present book.

Not only does the *Zohar*, as we have seen, teach the emanation of a threefold soul, but it also propounds a curious theory about the emanation of a pre-existent form or type of body, which, in the case of each one of us, unites the soul with the body. It is one of the strangest pieces of Zoharic psychology extant; and the object is probably that of accounting, on one and the same ground, for the varying physical and psychical characteristics embedded in each of us from birth. The passage runs as follows :

" At the moment when the earthly union [*i.e.* marriage] takes place, the Holy One (blessed be He) sends to earth a form [or image] resembling a man, and bearing upon itself the divine seal. This image is present at the moment just mentioned, and if the eye could see what goes on then, it would detect above the heads [of man and wife] an image like a human face, and this image is the model after which we are fashioned. . . . It is this image which receives us first on our arrival into this world. It grows in us as we grow, and leaves us when we leave the world. *This image is from above.* When the souls are about to quit their heavenly abode each soul appears before the Holy One (blessed be He) clothed with an exalted pattern [or image or form] on which are engraven the features which it will bear here below " (iii. 107).

But of far greater consequence in the history of Jewish mysticism is the commanding place assigned by the *Zohar* to the idea of Love. Indeed, Jewish mysticism is here but a reflection of the nature of the mysticism inherent in all other creeds. The soul's most visible, most tangible, most perceivable quality is love. The soul is the root of love. Love is the symbol of the soul. " Mystic Love," says Miss Underhill, " is the off-spring of the Celestial Venus ; the deep-seated desire and tendency of the soul towards its source." The soul, says the mystic of all ages, seeks to enter consciously into the Presence of God. It can do so only under the spur of an overpowering ecstatic emotion called love. Although, according to the *Zohar*, the soul in its most exalted state as *Neshāmāh* can only enjoy the love inherent

in its union with its source after it has freed
itself from the contamination of earthly
bodies, it is nevertheless possible, under certain conditions, to realise this ecstatic love
while the soul is in the living body of an
individual.   One of these conditions is *the
act of serving God*, the chief outward con-
comitant of which is *prayer*.

" Whosoever serves God out of love," says
the *Zohar*, " comes into union (*itdabak*) with
the place of the Highest of the High, and
comes into union, too, with the holiness of
the world which is to be " (ii. 216).   This is
to say that the service of God, when effected
with love, leads the soul into union with the
place of its origin, and it gives it, as it were, a
foretaste of the ineffable felicity which awaits
it in its highest condition as *Neshāmāh*.

The verse " Hear, O Israel, the Lord our
God the Lord is One " (*Deut*. vi. 4) hints, says
the *Zohar*, at this blending of the soul into a
Unity.   For this branch of its teaching the
Zohar is certainly not indebted to Neoplatonism or any other alien system.   It got
it from its Jewish predecessors—the Midrashic
homilists who enriched the Jewish literature
of the opening centuries of the Christian era
with their mystic interpretations of the
Song of Songs.   Verses like " I am my
beloved's, and my beloved is mine " (vi. 3)
served them as a starting-point for their
sermons on the nearness of man and God to

one another, brought about by the instrumentality of love.

When the soul has completed the cycle of its earthly career and hurries back to become blended with the Oversoul, it revels in ecstasies of love, which the *Zohar* describes with a wealth of poetic phraseology. The soul is received in what is termed a ' treasury of life,' or sometimes a ' temple of love,' and one of its crowning joys is to contemplate the Divine Presence through a ' shining mirror.' The Rabbis of the Talmud and Midrashim used the same phrase. Thus a passage in *Leviticus Rabba,* i. 14, reads thus : " All the other prophets saw God through nine shining mirrors, but Moses saw Him through only one. All the other prophets saw God through a blurred mirror, but Moses saw Him through a clear one." The meaning is that Moses had a clearer and nearer apprehension of the Deity than all other prophets.

Thus we read : " Come and see ! When the souls have reached the treasury of life they enjoy the shining of the brilliant mirror whose focus is in the heavens. And such is the brightness which emanates therefrom that the souls would be unable to withstand it, were they not covered with a coat of light. Even Moses could not approach it until he had stripped off his earthly integument " (i. 66). Again : " In one of the most mysterious and exalted parts of heaven, there is a

palace called the Palace of Love. Deep
mysteries are enacted there ; there are
gathered together all the most well-beloved
souls of the Heavenly King ; it is there that
the Heavenly King, the Holy One (blessed be
He), lives together with these holy souls and
unites Himself to them by kisses of love "
(ii. 97).

The Talmudic Rabbis described the way
in which death comes to the righteous as
' death by a kiss.' The *Zohar* defines this
' kiss ' as ' the union of the soul with its
root ' (i. 168). There is, in fine, an exceptionally high degree of optimism encircling
the *Zohar's* treatment of the soul.

If the theology of the early Rabbinic
schools of Palestine and Babylon errs, as
its critics say, in the direction of making
Judaism too much of a rigid discipline, too
much of a law-compelling, outward obedience rather than inward feeling, the balance
is redressed by the theology of the *Zohar*
which, by making the soul, on the completion
of its earthly work, so great a partaker in
the Divine love, emphasises the deep spirituality inherent in Judaism, the emotional
element which it calls forth in those who
rightfully and adequately put its teachings
into practice. It thus imports an added
brightness into Jewish life. It inspires the
Jew with the conviction that a high destiny
awaits him in the hereafter. It makes him

put a premium upon virtue, and encourages him to raise himself to the sublimest pitch of moral and religious worth. Judaism for the Jew can never be a mere soulless formalism so long as the *Zohar's* doctrine of Divine love is an integral part of Judaism. Such a consummation is well attested by such a passage from the *Zohar* as the following :

" When Adam our first father dwelt in the garden of Eden he was clothed, as men are in heaven, with the Divine light. When he was driven forth from Eden to do the ordinary work of earth, then Holy Writ tells us that ' the Lord God made for Adam and for his wife coats of skin and clothed them.' For, ere this, they wore coats of light, of that light which belongs to Eden.[1] Man's good deeds upon earth bring down on him a portion of the higher light which lights up heaven. It is that light which covers him like a coat when he enters into the future world and appears before his Maker, the Holy One (blessed be He). It is by means of such a covering that he can taste of the enjoyments of the elect and look upon the face of the ' shining mirror.' And thus, the soul, in order to become perfect in all respects, must have a different covering for each of the two

[1] In Hebrew there is a great similarity in sound between the word for ' skin ' and the word for ' light.'

worlds which it has to inhabit, one for the terrestrial world and the other for the higher world " (ii. 229).

And this cheerful view of the soul is an incitement to nobler effort, not only for the Jew as an individual, but also for the Jew as a unit of a race which, according to Scriptural prescription, looks forward to its highest evolution in the arrival of a Messiah. The *Zohar*, truly enough, is comparatively silent upon this theme. But the famous Kabbalist and mystic Isaac Luria, who is the chief expounder of the *Zohar*, and who carried many of its undeveloped dogmas to their logical conclusions, has elaborated this point in a strikingly ingenious and original way. Luria held a peculiar theory of the transmigration of the soul ; and conjoined with this there went, what might appear to some, an approach to Christian teaching about the truth of original sin. With the *Zohar*, Luria maintained that man, by means of his soul, unites the upper and the lower world. But he maintained further that with the creation of Adam there were created at the same time all the souls of all races of mankind. Just as there are variations in the physical qualities of men, so there are corresponding variations in their souls. Hence there are souls which are good and souls which are bad and souls of all the shades of value which lie between these two ex-

tremes. When Adam sinned there was confusion in all these classes of souls. The good
souls became tainted with some of the evil
inherent in the bad souls, and, on the contrary, the bad souls received many an
admixture of goodness from the superior
souls.

But who emanated from the inferior sets
of soul ? According to Luria, the pagan
world. Israel, however, issued from the
superior souls. But, again, seeing that the
good souls are not wholly good nor the bad
souls wholly bad by reason of the confusion
ensuing upon Adam's fall, it follows that
there can be no real unalloyed good in the
world. Evil infests some spot or other
everywhere. A perfect condition of things
will only come with the coming of the
Messiah. Until that time, therefore, all
souls, tainted as they all inevitably are with
sin, must, by means of a chain of transmigrations from one body to another, shake
off more and more of the dross clinging to
them, until they reach that summit of purity
and perfection when, as *Neshāmāh*, they can
find their way back to unite with the Infinite
Source, the Oversoul. Hence the individual
Jew in promoting the growth of his own soul
is really promoting the collective welfare
of his race. Upon the weal or woe of
his own soul hangs the weal or woe of his
people.

Luria's arguments, when fully stated, have a decided air of the fantastic about them. But that his conclusion is sound and valuable, no one will doubt. He encourages the Jew to the pursuit of a lofty communal or national ideal. He reminds him, too, of the imperative necessity of Israel's solidarity. For the Jew, taking his stand upon many a text in the Old Testament, has always felt that his thought and his work must not be for himself alone. His prayer has ever been for the well-being of Israel rather than for the well-being of individual Israelites. What he counts, in God's sight, as a separate entity is small in comparison with what he counts as an inseparable unit in the compact body of Israel. In this voluntary, self-forgetful merging of the smaller interests of the part in the greater interests of the whole lies much of the secret of the long roll of Israel's saints and heroes, his martyrs and his mystics.

CONCLUDING NOTE

THE course of Jewish mysticism subsequent
to the *Zohar* consists, in the main, of develop-
ments and elaborations, by Jews in many
lands, of the doctrines taught in that unique
work. There is an enormous fund of origin-
ality in many of these elaborations. Their
writers were men engrained with the deepest
of mystical sentiments, men whose lives
accorded with the high strain of their teachings, and whose writings constitute a material
addition, for all time, to the body of Jewish
spiritual literature. But limits of space
prevent the consideration of this subject.
At the beginning of the eighteenth century
there arose, among the Jews of Poland,
a great religious movement known as
' Ḥasidism ' (from Hebrew *ḥasid* = pious).
Its aim was to revive the spiritual element in
Judaism which had been largely crushed
out of existence by the dead - weight of
Rabbinical formalism. Ḥasidism was in-
vented in order to show that Judaism meant
not merely law and commandment, ritual
and dogma, but denoted also the emotions
of love and aspiration and faith felt towards

a Father who was eternally near, and whose heart overflowed with a father's compassion for his children. Hasidism strove to effect for Judaism the supremacy of inward ' first-hand ' religion over the dogmatism of outward traditionalism. Judaism needed this corrective. And although Hasidism is often flouted as a failure, and its adherents depreciated as the devotees of excess and extravagance in religious exercise, it nevertheless was a force, and deserves an abiding place in the history of Jewish theology, if only on the ground that it tried to do for Judaism what the general mystical tendencies of our own day are more and more doing for it, *viz.* to make it conscious of how dominating a part is played in it by the inner impulse urging us to seek and to find a pathway to the realised Presence of God.

BIBLIOGRAPHY

WORKS in English are unfortunately very few. On the whole subject of the mystical elements in Talmudic, Midrashic, and Kabbalistic theology, the student should see :

A. Franck, *La Kabbale* (Paris, 1843 ; 2nd ed., 1889). German Trans. (with many original additions) by A. Jellinek (Leipsic, 1844).

Ginsburg, *The Kabbalah* (London, 1865).

Isaac Myer, *Qabbalah* (Philadelphia, 1888).

Karppe, *Étude sur les Origines et la Nature du Zohar* (Paris, 1901).

Joël, 'Essays on Ibn Gabirol,' in his *Beiträge zur Geschichte der Philosophie*, 1876.

All of the above works contain many translations of the original Hebrew and Aramaic.

On the subject of the Essenes :

Graetz, *History of the Jews* (English Trans., vol. ii. pp. 16–34).

Ginsburg, *The Essenes, their History and their Doctrines* (London, 1864).

Article ' Essenes ' by F. C. Conybeare in Hastings' *Dictionary of the Bible.*

Article ' Essenes ' in *Jewish Encyclopædia.*

Philo's *The Contemplative Life*, ed. Conybeare (Oxford, 1895).

On the Jewish Hellenistic Literature :

Schürer, *Geschichte des Jüdischen Volkes im Zeitalter Jesu Christi*, ii. pp. 556–584.
Freudenthal, *Hellenistische Studien*, 1879.
Gerald Friedlander, *Hellenism and Christianity* (London, 1912).
C. G. Montefiore, *The Wisdom of Solomon* (London, 1891).

On Philo :

Drummond, *Philo Judœus* (London, 1888).

On Shechinah, Memra, Holy Spirit :

Volz, *Der Geist Gottes* (Tübingen, 1910).
Abelson, *The Immanence of God in Rabbinical Literature* (London, 1912).

On the *Yetsīrah* book :

Franck, *La Kabbale*, pp. 53–66, 102–118.
Graetz, *Gnosticismus und Judenthum* (Breslau, 1846), pp. 102–132.
  Parts of it are translated into English in W. W. Westcott's *Sefer Yezirah* (London, 1893) and into French in Karppe's *Étude sur les Origines et la Nature du Zohar* (Paris, 1901).

On the doctrines of Emanation and the Ten Sefirot :

Joël, in the work previously mentioned. It contains the best account of the relation between Jewish and Neoplatonic mysticism.
Ehrenpreis, *Die Entwickelung der Emanationslehre in der Kabbalah des XIII. Jahrhunderts* (Frankfurt, 1895). This work is indispens-

able for the history of the development of ideas.

Éliphaz Lévi, *Le Livre des Splendeurs* (Paris, 1894).

A translation of the whole of the *Zohar*, into French, by the late Jean de Pauly, has recently been published. It is absolutely indispensable as the only complete translation yet attempted.

INDEX

A CATALOG OF SELECTED DOVER
BOOKS IN ALL FIELDS OF INTEREST

CONCERNING THE SPIRITUAL IN ART, Wassily Kandinsky. Pioneering work by father of abstract art. Thoughts on color theory, nature of art. Analysis of earlier masters. 12 illustrations. 80pp. of text. 5⅜ x 8½.   23411-8 Pa. $4.95

ANIMALS: 1,419 Copyright-Free Illustrations of Mammals, Birds, Fish, Insects, etc., Jim Harter (ed.). Clear wood engravings present, in extremely lifelike poses, over 1,000 species of animals. One of the most extensive pictorial sourcebooks of its kind. Captions. Index. 284pp. 9 x 12.   23766-4 Pa. $14.95

CELTIC ART: The Methods of Construction, George Bain. Simple geometric techniques for making Celtic interlacements, spirals, Kells-type initials, animals, humans, etc. Over 500 illustrations. 160pp. 9 x 12. (Available in U.S. only.)   22923-8 Pa. $9.95

AN ATLAS OF ANATOMY FOR ARTISTS, Fritz Schider. Most thorough reference work on art anatomy in the world. Hundreds of illustrations, including selections from works by Vesalius, Leonardo, Goya, Ingres, Michelangelo, others. 593 illustrations. 192pp. 7⅛ x 10¼.   20241-0 Pa. $9.95

CELTIC HAND STROKE-BY-STROKE (Irish Half-Uncial from "The Book of Kells"): An Arthur Baker Calligraphy Manual, Arthur Baker. Complete guide to creating each letter of the alphabet in distinctive Celtic manner. Covers hand position, strokes, pens, inks, paper, more. Illustrated. 48pp. 8¼ x 11.   24336-2 Pa. $3.95

EASY ORIGAMI, John Montroll. Charming collection of 32 projects (hat, cup, pelican, piano, swan, many more) specially designed for the novice origami hobbyist. Clearly illustrated easy-to-follow instructions insure that even beginning papercrafters will achieve successful results. 48pp. 8¼ x 11.   27298-2 Pa. $3.50

THE COMPLETE BOOK OF BIRDHOUSE CONSTRUCTION FOR WOODWORKERS, Scott D. Campbell. Detailed instructions, illustrations, tables. Also data on bird habitat and instinct patterns. Bibliography. 3 tables. 63 illustrations in 15 figures. 48pp. 5¼ x 8½.   24407-5 Pa. $2.50

BLOOMINGDALE'S ILLUSTRATED 1886 CATALOG: Fashions, Dry Goods and Housewares, Bloomingdale Brothers. Famed merchants' extremely rare catalog depicting about 1,700 products: clothing, housewares, firearms, dry goods, jewelry, more. Invaluable for dating, identifying vintage items. Also, copyright-free graphics for artists, designers. Co-published with Henry Ford Museum & Greenfield Village. 160pp. 8¼ x 11.   25780-0 Pa. $12.95

HISTORIC COSTUME IN PICTURES, Braun & Schneider. Over 1,450 costumed figures in clearly detailed engravings–from dawn of civilization to end of 19th century. Captions. Many folk costumes. 256pp. 8⅜ x 11¾.   23150-X Pa. $12.95

STICKLEY CRAFTSMAN FURNITURE CATALOGS, Gustav Stickley and L. & J. G. Stickley. Beautiful, functional furniture in two authentic catalogs from 1910. 594 illustrations, including 277 photos, show settles, rockers, armchairs, reclining chairs, bookcases, desks, tables. 183pp. 6½ x 9¼. 23838-5 Pa. $11.95

AMERICAN LOCOMOTIVES IN HISTORIC PHOTOGRAPHS: 1858 to 1949, Ron Ziel (ed.). A rare collection of 126 meticulously detailed official photographs, called "builder portraits," of American locomotives that majestically chronicle the rise of steam locomotive power in America. Introduction. Detailed captions. xi+ 129pp. 9 x 12. 27393-8 Pa. $13.95

AMERICA'S LIGHTHOUSES: An Illustrated History, Francis Ross Holland, Jr. Delightfully written, profusely illustrated fact-filled survey of over 200 American lighthouses since 1716. History, anecdotes, technological advances, more. 240pp. 8 x 10¾. 25576-X Pa. $12.95

TOWARDS A NEW ARCHITECTURE, Le Corbusier. Pioneering manifesto by founder of "International School." Technical and aesthetic theories, views of industry, economics, relation of form to function, "mass-production split" and much more. Profusely illustrated. 320pp. 6⅛ x 9¼. (Available in U.S. only.) 25023-7 Pa. $10.95

HOW THE OTHER HALF LIVES, Jacob Riis. Famous journalistic record, exposing poverty and degradation of New York slums around 1900, by major social reformer. 100 striking and influential photographs. 233pp. 10 x 7⅞. 22012-5 Pa. $11.95

FRUIT KEY AND TWIG KEY TO TREES AND SHRUBS, William M. Harlow. One of the handiest and most widely used identification aids. Fruit key covers 120 deciduous and evergreen species; twig key 160 deciduous species. Easily used. Over 300 photographs. 126pp. 5⅜ x 8½. 20511-8 Pa. $3.95

COMMON BIRD SONGS, Dr. Donald J. Borror. Songs of 60 most common U.S. birds: robins, sparrows, cardinals, bluejays, finches, more—arranged in order of increasing complexity. Up to 9 variations of songs of each species.
Cassette and manual 99911-4 $8.95

ORCHIDS AS HOUSE PLANTS, Rebecca Tyson Northen. Grow cattleyas and many other kinds of orchids—in a window, in a case, or under artificial light. 63 illustrations. 148pp. 5⅜ x 8½. 23261-1 Pa. $7.95

MONSTER MAZES, Dave Phillips. Masterful mazes at four levels of difficulty. Avoid deadly perils and evil creatures to find magical treasures. Solutions for all 32 exciting illustrated puzzles. 48pp. 8¼ x 11. 26005-4 Pa. $2.95

MOZART'S DON GIOVANNI (DOVER OPERA LIBRETTO SERIES), Wolfgang Amadeus Mozart. Introduced and translated by Ellen H. Bleiler. Standard Italian libretto, with complete English translation. Convenient and thoroughly portable—an ideal companion for reading along with a recording or the performance itself. Introduction. List of characters. Plot summary. 121pp. 5¼ x 8½. 24944-1 Pa. $3.95

TECHNICAL MANUAL AND DICTIONARY OF CLASSICAL BALLET, Gail Grant. Defines, explains, comments on steps, movements, poses and concepts. 15-page pictorial section. Basic book for student, viewer. 127pp. 5⅜ x 8½. 21843-0 Pa. $4.95

THE CLARINET AND CLARINET PLAYING, David Pino. Lively, comprehensive work features suggestions about technique, musicianship, and musical interpretation, as well as guidelines for teaching, making your own reeds, and preparing for public performance. Includes an intriguing look at clarinet history. "A godsend," *The Clarinet*, Journal of the International Clarinet Society. Appendixes. 7 illus. 320pp. 5⅜ x 8½. 40270-3 Pa. $9.95

HOLLYWOOD GLAMOR PORTRAITS, John Kobal (ed.). 145 photos from 1926-49. Harlow, Gable, Bogart, Bacall; 94 stars in all. Full background on photographers, technical aspects. 160pp. 8⅜ x 11¼. 23352-9 Pa. $12.95

THE ANNOTATED CASEY AT THE BAT: A Collection of Ballads about the Mighty Casey/Third, Revised Edition, Martin Gardner (ed.). Amusing sequels and parodies of one of America's best-loved poems: Casey's Revenge, Why Casey Whiffed, Casey's Sister at the Bat, others. 256pp. 5⅜ x 8½. 28598-7 Pa. $8.95

THE RAVEN AND OTHER FAVORITE POEMS, Edgar Allan Poe. Over 40 of the author's most memorable poems: "The Bells," "Ulalume," "Israfel," "To Helen," "The Conqueror Worm," "Eldorado," "Annabel Lee," many more. Alphabetic lists of titles and first lines. 64pp. 5$\frac{3}{16}$ x 8¼. 26685-0 Pa. $1.00

PERSONAL MEMOIRS OF U. S. GRANT, Ulysses Simpson Grant. Intelligent, deeply moving firsthand account of Civil War campaigns, considered by many the finest military memoirs ever written. Includes letters, historic photographs, maps and more. 528pp. 6⅛ x 9¼. 28587-1 Pa. $12.95

ANCIENT EGYPTIAN MATERIALS AND INDUSTRIES, A. Lucas and J. Harris. Fascinating, comprehensive, thoroughly documented text describes this ancient civilization's vast resources and the processes that incorporated them in daily life, including the use of animal products, building materials, cosmetics, perfumes and incense, fibers, glazed ware, glass and its manufacture, materials used in the mummification process, and much more. 544pp. 6⅛ x 9¼. (Available in U.S. only.) 40446-3 Pa. $16.95

RUSSIAN STORIES/PYCCKNE PACCKA3bl: A Dual-Language Book, edited by Gleb Struve. Twelve tales by such masters as Chekhov, Tolstoy, Dostoevsky, Pushkin, others. Excellent word-for-word English translations on facing pages, plus teaching and study aids, Russian/English vocabulary, biographical/critical introductions, more. 416pp. 5⅜ x 8½. 26244-8 Pa. $9.95

PHILADELPHIA THEN AND NOW: 60 Sites Photographed in the Past and Present, Kenneth Finkel and Susan Oyama. Rare photographs of City Hall, Logan Square, Independence Hall, Betsy Ross House, other landmarks juxtaposed with contemporary views. Captures changing face of historic city. Introduction. Captions. 128pp. 8¼ x 11. 25790-8 Pa. $9.95

AIA ARCHITECTURAL GUIDE TO NASSAU AND SUFFOLK COUNTIES, LONG ISLAND, The American Institute of Architects, Long Island Chapter, and the Society for the Preservation of Long Island Antiquities. Comprehensive, well-researched and generously illustrated volume brings to life over three centuries of Long Island's great architectural heritage. More than 240 photographs with authoritative, extensively detailed captions. 176pp. 8¼ x 11. 26946-9 Pa. $14.95

NORTH AMERICAN INDIAN LIFE: Customs and Traditions of 23 Tribes, Elsie Clews Parsons (ed.). 27 fictionalized essays by noted anthropologists examine religion, customs, government, additional facets of life among the Winnebago, Crow, Zuni, Eskimo, other tribes. 480pp. 6⅛ x 9¼. 27377-6 Pa. $10.95

FRANK LLOYD WRIGHT'S DANA HOUSE, Donald Hoffmann. Pictorial essay of residential masterpiece with over 160 interior and exterior photos, plans, elevations, sketches and studies. 128pp. 9¼ x 10¾. 29120-0 Pa. $14.95

THE MALE AND FEMALE FIGURE IN MOTION: 60 Classic Photographic Sequences, Eadweard Muybridge. 60 true-action photographs of men and women walking, running, climbing, bending, turning, etc., reproduced from rare 19th-century masterpiece. vi + 121pp. 9 x 12. 24745-7 Pa. $12.95

1001 QUESTIONS ANSWERED ABOUT THE SEASHORE, N. J. Berrill and Jacquelyn Berrill. Queries answered about dolphins, sea snails, sponges, starfish, fishes, shore birds, many others. Covers appearance, breeding, growth, feeding, much more. 305pp. 5¼ x 8¼. 23366-9 Pa. $9.95

ATTRACTING BIRDS TO YOUR YARD, William J. Weber. Easy-to-follow guide offers advice on how to attract the greatest diversity of birds: birdhouses, feeders, water and waterers, much more. 96pp. 5³⁄₁₆ x 8¼. 28927-3 Pa. $2.50

MEDICINAL AND OTHER USES OF NORTH AMERICAN PLANTS: A Historical Survey with Special Reference to the Eastern Indian Tribes, Charlotte Erichsen-Brown. Chronological historical citations document 500 years of usage of plants, trees, shrubs native to eastern Canada, northeastern U.S. Also complete identifying information. 343 illustrations. 544pp. 6½ x 9¼. 25951-X Pa. $12.95

STORYBOOK MAZES, Dave Phillips. 23 stories and mazes on two-page spreads: Wizard of Oz, Treasure Island, Robin Hood, etc. Solutions. 64pp. 8¼ x 11. 23628-5 Pa. $2.95

AMERICAN NEGRO SONGS: 230 Folk Songs and Spirituals, Religious and Secular, John W. Work. This authoritative study traces the African influences of songs sung and played by black Americans at work, in church, and as entertainment. The author discusses the lyric significance of such songs as "Swing Low, Sweet Chariot," "John Henry," and others and offers the words and music for 230 songs. Bibliography. Index of Song Titles. 272pp. 6½ x 9¼. 40271-1 Pa. $10.95

MOVIE-STAR PORTRAITS OF THE FORTIES, John Kobal (ed.). 163 glamor, studio photos of 106 stars of the 1940s: Rita Hayworth, Ava Gardner, Marlon Brando, Clark Gable, many more. 176pp. 8⅜ x 11¼. 23546-7 Pa. $14.95

BENCHLEY LOST AND FOUND, Robert Benchley. Finest humor from early 30s, about pet peeves, child psychologists, post office and others. Mostly unavailable elsewhere. 73 illustrations by Peter Arno and others. 183pp. 5⅜ x 8½. 22410-4 Pa. $6.95

YEKL and THE IMPORTED BRIDEGROOM AND OTHER STORIES OF YIDDISH NEW YORK, Abraham Cahan. Film Hester Street based on *Yekl* (1896). Novel, other stories among first about Jewish immigrants on N.Y.'s East Side. 240pp. 5⅜ x 8½. 22427-9 Pa. $7.95

SELECTED POEMS, Walt Whitman. Generous sampling from *Leaves of Grass*. Twenty-four poems include "I Hear America Singing," "Song of the Open Road," "I Sing the Body Electric," "When Lilacs Last in the Dooryard Bloom'd," "O Captain! My Captain!"–all reprinted from an authoritative edition. Lists of titles and first lines. 128pp. 5³⁄₁₆ x 8¼. 26878-0 Pa. $1.00

CATALOG OF DOVER BOOKS

THE BEST TALES OF HOFFMANN, E. T. A. Hoffmann. 10 of Hoffmann's most important stories: "Nutcracker and the King of Mice," "The Golden Flowerpot," etc. 458pp. 5⅜ x 8½. 21793-0 Pa. $9.95

FROM FETISH TO GOD IN ANCIENT EGYPT, E. A. Wallis Budge. Rich detailed survey of Egyptian conception of "God" and gods, magic, cult of animals, Osiris, more. Also, superb English translations of hymns and legends. 240 illustrations. 545pp. 5⅜ x 8½. 25803-3 Pa. $13.95

FRENCH STORIES/CONTES FRANÇAIS: A Dual-Language Book, Wallace Fowlie. Ten stories by French masters, Voltaire to Camus: "Micromegas" by Voltaire; "The Atheist's Mass" by Balzac; "Minuet" by de Maupassant; "The Guest" by Camus, six more. Excellent English translations on facing pages. Also French-English vocabulary list, exercises, more. 352pp. 5⅜ x 8½. 26443-2 Pa. $9.95

CHICAGO AT THE TURN OF THE CENTURY IN PHOTOGRAPHS: 122 Historic Views from the Collections of the Chicago Historical Society, Larry A. Viskochil. Rare large-format prints offer detailed views of City Hall, State Street, the Loop, Hull House, Union Station, many other landmarks, circa 1904-1913. Introduction. Captions. Maps. 144pp. 9⅜ x 12¼. 24656-6 Pa. $12.95

OLD BROOKLYN IN EARLY PHOTOGRAPHS, 1865-1929, William Lee Younger. Luna Park, Gravesend race track, construction of Grand Army Plaza, moving of Hotel Brighton, etc. 157 previously unpublished photographs. 165pp. 8⅞ x 11¾. 23587-4 Pa. $13.95

THE MYTHS OF THE NORTH AMERICAN INDIANS, Lewis Spence. Rich anthology of the myths and legends of the Algonquins, Iroquois, Pawnees and Sioux, prefaced by an extensive historical and ethnological commentary. 36 illustrations. 480pp. 5⅜ x 8½. 25967-6 Pa. $10.95

AN ENCYCLOPEDIA OF BATTLES: Accounts of Over 1,560 Battles from 1479 B.C. to the Present, David Eggenberger. Essential details of every major battle in recorded history from the first battle of Megiddo in 1479 B.C. to Grenada in 1984. List of Battle Maps. New Appendix covering the years 1967-1984. Index. 99 illustrations. 544pp. 6½ x 9¼. 24913-1 Pa. $16.95

SAILING ALONE AROUND THE WORLD, Captain Joshua Slocum. First man to sail around the world, alone, in small boat. One of great feats of seamanship told in delightful manner. 67 illustrations. 294pp. 5⅜ x 8½. 20326-3 Pa. $6.95

ANARCHISM AND OTHER ESSAYS, Emma Goldman. Powerful, penetrating, prophetic essays on direct action, role of minorities, prison reform, puritan hypocrisy, violence, etc. 271pp. 5⅜ x 8½. 22484-8 Pa. $8.95

MYTHS OF THE HINDUS AND BUDDHISTS, Ananda K. Coomaraswamy and Sister Nivedita. Great stories of the epics; deeds of Krishna, Shiva, taken from puranas, Vedas, folk tales; etc. 32 illustrations. 400pp. 5⅜ x 8½. 21759-0 Pa. $12.95

THE TRAUMA OF BIRTH, Otto Rank. Rank's controversial thesis that anxiety neurosis is caused by profound psychological trauma which occurs at birth. 256pp. 5⅜ x 8½. 27974-X Pa. $7.95

A THEOLOGICO-POLITICAL TREATISE, Benedict Spinoza. Also contains unfinished Political Treatise. Great classic on religious liberty, theory of government on common consent. R. Elwes translation. Total of 421pp. 5⅜ x 8½. 20249-6 Pa. $10.95

MY BONDAGE AND MY FREEDOM, Frederick Douglass. Born a slave, Douglass became outspoken force in antislavery movement. The best of Douglass' autobiographies. Graphic description of slave life. 464pp. 5⅜ x 8½. 22457-0 Pa. $8.95

FOLLOWING THE EQUATOR: A Journey Around the World, Mark Twain. Fascinating humorous account of 1897 voyage to Hawaii, Australia, India, New Zealand, etc. Ironic, bemused reports on peoples, customs, climate, flora and fauna, politics, much more. 197 illustrations. 720pp. 5⅜ x 8½. 26113-1 Pa. $15.95

THE PEOPLE CALLED SHAKERS, Edward D. Andrews. Definitive study of Shakers: origins, beliefs, practices, dances, social organization, furniture and crafts, etc. 33 illustrations. 351pp. 5⅜ x 8½. 21081-2 Pa. $12.95

THE MYTHS OF GREECE AND ROME, H. A. Guerber. A classic of mythology, generously illustrated, long prized for its simple, graphic, accurate retelling of the principal myths of Greece and Rome, and for its commentary on their origins and significance. With 64 illustrations by Michelangelo, Raphael, Titian, Rubens, Canova, Bernini and others. 480pp. 5⅜ x 8½. 27584-1 Pa. $10.95

PSYCHOLOGY OF MUSIC, Carl E. Seashore. Classic work discusses music as a medium from psychological viewpoint. Clear treatment of physical acoustics, auditory apparatus, sound perception, development of musical skills, nature of musical feeling, host of other topics. 88 figures. 408pp. 5⅜ x 8½. 21851-1 Pa. $11.95

THE PHILOSOPHY OF HISTORY, Georg W. Hegel. Great classic of Western thought develops concept that history is not chance but rational process, the evolution of freedom. 457pp. 5⅜ x 8½. 20112-0 Pa. $9.95

THE BOOK OF TEA, Kakuzo Okakura. Minor classic of the Orient: entertaining, charming explanation, interpretation of traditional Japanese culture in terms of tea ceremony. 94pp. 5⅜ x 8½. 20070-1 Pa. $3.95

LIFE IN ANCIENT EGYPT, Adolf Erman. Fullest, most thorough, detailed older account with much not in more recent books, domestic life, religion, magic, medicine, commerce, much more. Many illustrations reproduce tomb paintings, carvings, hieroglyphs, etc. 597pp. 5⅜ x 8½. 22632-8 Pa. $12.95

SUNDIALS, Their Theory and Construction, Albert Waugh. Far and away the best, most thorough coverage of ideas, mathematics concerned, types, construction, adjusting anywhere. Simple, nontechnical treatment allows even children to build several of these dials. Over 100 illustrations. 230pp. 5⅜ x 8½. 22947-5 Pa. $8.95

THEORETICAL HYDRODYNAMICS, L. M. Milne-Thomson. Classic exposition of the mathematical theory of fluid motion, applicable to both hydrodynamics and aerodynamics. Over 600 exercises. 768pp. 6⅛ x 9¼. 68970-0 Pa. $20.95

SONGS OF EXPERIENCE: Facsimile Reproduction with 26 Plates in Full Color, William Blake. 26 full-color plates from a rare 1826 edition. Includes "TheTyger," "London," "Holy Thursday," and other poems. Printed text of poems. 48pp. 5¼ x 7. 24636-1 Pa. $4.95

OLD-TIME VIGNETTES IN FULL COLOR, Carol Belanger Grafton (ed.). Over 390 charming, often sentimental illustrations, selected from archives of Victorian graphics—pretty women posing, children playing, food, flowers, kittens and puppies, smiling cherubs, birds and butterflies, much more. All copyright-free. 48pp. 9¼ x 12¼. 27269-9 Pa. $9.95

PERSPECTIVE FOR ARTISTS, Rex Vicat Cole. Depth, perspective of sky and sea, shadows, much more, not usually covered. 391 diagrams, 81 reproductions of drawings and paintings. 279pp. 5⅜ x 8½. 22487-2 Pa. $9.95

DRAWING THE LIVING FIGURE, Joseph Sheppard. Innovative approach to artistic anatomy focuses on specifics of surface anatomy, rather than muscles and bones. Over 170 drawings of live models in front, back and side views, and in widely varying poses. Accompanying diagrams. 177 illustrations. Introduction. Index. 144pp. 8⅜ x11¼. 26723-7 Pa. $9.95

GOTHIC AND OLD ENGLISH ALPHABETS: 100 Complete Fonts, Dan X. Solo. Add power, elegance to posters, signs, other graphics with 100 stunning copyright-free alphabets: Blackstone, Dolbey, Germania, 97 more–including many lower-case, numerals, punctuation marks. 104pp. 8⅛ x 11. 24695-7 Pa. $9.95

HOW TO DO BEADWORK, Mary White. Fundamental book on craft from simple projects to five-bead chains and woven works. 106 illustrations. 142pp. 5⅜ x 8. 20697-1 Pa. $5.95

THE BOOK OF WOOD CARVING, Charles Marshall Sayers. Finest book for beginners discusses fundamentals and offers 34 designs. "Absolutely first rate . . . well thought out and well executed."–E. J. Tangerman. 118pp. 7¾ x 10⅝. 23654-4 Pa. $7.95

ILLUSTRATED CATALOG OF CIVIL WAR MILITARY GOODS: Union Army Weapons, Insignia, Uniform Accessories, and Other Equipment, Schuyler, Hartley, and Graham. Rare, profusely illustrated 1846 catalog includes Union Army uniform and dress regulations, arms and ammunition, coats, insignia, flags, swords, rifles, etc. 226 illustrations. 160pp. 9 x 12. 24939-5 Pa. $12.95

WOMEN'S FASHIONS OF THE EARLY 1900s: An Unabridged Republication of "New York Fashions, 1909," National Cloak & Suit Co. Rare catalog of mail-order fashions documents women's and children's clothing styles shortly after the turn of the century. Captions offer full descriptions, prices. Invaluable resource for fashion, costume historians. Approximately 725 illustrations. 128pp. 8⅜ x 11¼. 27276-1 Pa. $12.95

THE 1912 AND 1915 GUSTAV STICKLEY FURNITURE CATALOGS, Gustav Stickley. With over 200 detailed illustrations and descriptions, these two catalogs are essential reading and reference materials and identification guides for Stickley furniture. Captions cite materials, dimensions and prices. 112pp. 6½ x 9¼. 26676-1 Pa. $9.95

EARLY AMERICAN LOCOMOTIVES, John H. White, Jr. Finest locomotive engravings from early 19th century: historical (1804–74), main-line (after 1870), special, foreign, etc. 147 plates. 142pp. 11⅜ x 8¼. 22772-3 Pa. $12.95

THE TALL SHIPS OF TODAY IN PHOTOGRAPHS, Frank O. Braynard. Lavishly illustrated tribute to nearly 100 majestic contemporary sailing vessels: Amerigo Vespucci, Clearwater, Constitution, Eagle, Mayflower, Sea Cloud, Victory, many more. Authoritative captions provide statistics, background on each ship. 190 black-and-white photographs and illustrations. Introduction. 128pp. 8⅞ x 11¾. 27163-3 Pa. $14.95

LITTLE BOOK OF EARLY AMERICAN CRAFTS AND TRADES, Peter Stockham (ed.). 1807 children's book explains crafts and trades: baker, hatter, cooper, potter, and many others. 23 copperplate illustrations. 140pp. 4⅝ x 6.
23336-7 Pa. $4.95

VICTORIAN FASHIONS AND COSTUMES FROM HARPER'S BAZAR, 1867–1898, Stella Blum (ed.). Day costumes, evening wear, sports clothes, shoes, hats, other accessories in over 1,000 detailed engravings. 320pp. 9⅜ x 12¼.
22990-4 Pa. $16.95

GUSTAV STICKLEY, THE CRAFTSMAN, Mary Ann Smith. Superb study surveys broad scope of Stickley's achievement, especially in architecture. Design philosophy, rise and fall of the Craftsman empire, descriptions and floor plans for many Craftsman houses, more. 86 black-and-white halftones. 31 line illustrations. Introduction 208pp. 6½ x 9¼. 27210-9 Pa. $9.95

THE LONG ISLAND RAIL ROAD IN EARLY PHOTOGRAPHS, Ron Ziel. Over 220 rare photos, informative text document origin (1844) and development of rail service on Long Island. Vintage views of early trains, locomotives, stations, passengers, crews, much more. Captions. 8¾ x 11¾. 26301-0 Pa. $14.95

VOYAGE OF THE LIBERDADE, Joshua Slocum. Great 19th-century mariner's thrilling, first-hand account of the wreck of his ship off South America, the 35-foot boat he built from the wreckage, and its remarkable voyage home. 128pp. 5⅜ x 8½.
40022-0 Pa. $5.95

TEN BOOKS ON ARCHITECTURE, Vitruvius. The most important book ever written on architecture. Early Roman aesthetics, technology, classical orders, site selection, all other aspects. Morgan translation. 331pp. 5⅜ x 8½. 20645-9 Pa. $9.95

THE HUMAN FIGURE IN MOTION, Eadweard Muybridge. More than 4,500 stopped-action photos, in action series, showing undraped men, women, children jumping, lying down, throwing, sitting, wrestling, carrying, etc. 390pp. 7⅞ x 10⅝.
20204-6 Clothbd. $29.95

TREES OF THE EASTERN AND CENTRAL UNITED STATES AND CANADA, William M. Harlow. Best one-volume guide to 140 trees. Full descriptions, woodlore, range, etc. Over 600 illustrations. Handy size. 288pp. 4½ x 6⅜.
20395-6 Pa. $6.95

SONGS OF WESTERN BIRDS, Dr. Donald J. Borror. Complete song and call repertoire of 60 western species, including flycatchers, juncoes, cactus wrens, many more—includes fully illustrated booklet. Cassette and manual 99913-0 $8.95

GROWING AND USING HERBS AND SPICES, Milo Miloradovich. Versatile handbook provides all the information needed for cultivation and use of all the herbs and spices available in North America. 4 illustrations. Index. Glossary. 236pp. 5⅜ x 8½.
25058-X Pa. $7.95

BIG BOOK OF MAZES AND LABYRINTHS, Walter Shepherd. 50 mazes and labyrinths in all—classical, solid, ripple, and more—in one great volume. Perfect inexpensive puzzler for clever youngsters. Full solutions. 112pp. 8⅛ x 11.
22951-3 Pa. $5.95

PIANO TUNING, J. Cree Fischer. Clearest, best book for beginner, amateur. Simple repairs, raising dropped notes, tuning by easy method of flattened fifths. No previous skills needed. 4 illustrations. 201pp. 5⅜ x 8½. 23267-0 Pa. $6.95

HINTS TO SINGERS, Lillian Nordica. Selecting the right teacher, developing confidence, overcoming stage fright, and many other important skills receive thoughtful discussion in this indispensible guide, written by a world-famous diva of four decades' experience. 96pp. 5⅜ x 8½. 40094-8 Pa. $4.95

THE COMPLETE NONSENSE OF EDWARD LEAR, Edward Lear. All nonsense limericks, zany alphabets, Owl and Pussycat, songs, nonsense botany, etc., illustrated by Lear. Total of 320pp. 5⅜ x 8½. (Available in U.S. only.) 20167-8 Pa. $7.95

VICTORIAN PARLOUR POETRY: An Annotated Anthology, Michael R. Turner. 117 gems by Longfellow, Tennyson, Browning, many lesser-known poets. "The Village Blacksmith," "Curfew Must Not Ring Tonight," "Only a Baby Small," dozens more, often difficult to find elsewhere. Index of poets, titles, first lines. xxiii + 325pp. 5⅝ x 8¼. 27044-0 Pa. $12.95

DUBLINERS, James Joyce. Fifteen stories offer vivid, tightly focused observations of the lives of Dublin's poorer classes. At least one, "The Dead," is considered a masterpiece. Reprinted complete and unabridged from standard edition. 160pp. 5³⁄₁₆ x 8¼. 26870-5 Pa. $1.50

GREAT WEIRD TALES: 14 Stories by Lovecraft, Blackwood, Machen and Others, S. T. Joshi (ed.). 14 spellbinding tales, including "The Sin Eater," by Fiona McLeod, "The Eye Above the Mantel," by Frank Belknap Long, as well as renowned works by R. H. Barlow, Lord Dunsany, Arthur Machen, W. C. Morrow and eight other masters of the genre. 256pp. 5⅜ x 8½. (Available in U.S. only.) 40436-6 Pa. $8.95

THE BOOK OF THE SACRED MAGIC OF ABRAMELIN THE MAGE, translated by S. MacGregor Mathers. Medieval manuscript of ceremonial magic. Basic document in Aleister Crowley, Golden Dawn groups. 268pp. 5⅜ x 8½. 23211-5 Pa. $9.95

NEW RUSSIAN-ENGLISH AND ENGLISH-RUSSIAN DICTIONARY, M. A. O'Brien. This is a remarkably handy Russian dictionary, containing a surprising amount of information, including over 70,000 entries. 366pp. 4½ x 6⅛. 20208-9 Pa. $10.95

HISTORIC HOMES OF THE AMERICAN PRESIDENTS, Second, Revised Edition, Irvin Haas. A traveler's guide to American Presidential homes, most open to the public, depicting and describing homes occupied by every American President from George Washington to George Bush. With visiting hours, admission charges, travel routes. 175 photographs. Index. 160pp. 8¼ x 11. 26751-2 Pa. $13.95

NEW YORK IN THE FORTIES, Andreas Feininger. 162 brilliant photographs by the well-known photographer, formerly with *Life* magazine. Commuters, shoppers, Times Square at night, much else from city at its peak. Captions by John von Hartz. 181pp. 9¼ x 10¾. 23585-8 Pa. $13.95

INDIAN SIGN LANGUAGE, William Tomkins. Over 525 signs developed by Sioux and other tribes. Written instructions and diagrams. Also 290 pictographs. 111pp. 6⅛ x 9¼. 22029-X Pa. $3.95

CATALOG OF DOVER BOOKS

ANATOMY: A Complete Guide for Artists, Joseph Sheppard. A master of figure drawing shows artists how to render human anatomy convincingly. Over 460 illustrations. 224pp. 8⅜ x 11¼. 27279-6 Pa. $11.95

MEDIEVAL CALLIGRAPHY: Its History and Technique, Marc Drogin. Spirited history, comprehensive instruction manual covers 13 styles (ca. 4th century through 15th). Excellent photographs; directions for duplicating medieval techniques with modern tools. 224pp. 8⅜ x 11¼. 26142-5 Pa. $12.95

DRIED FLOWERS: How to Prepare Them, Sarah Whitlock and Martha Rankin. Complete instructions on how to use silica gel, meal and borax, perlite aggregate, sand and borax, glycerine and water to create attractive permanent flower arrangements. 12 illustrations. 32pp. 5⅜ x 8½. 21802-3 Pa. $1.00

EASY-TO-MAKE BIRD FEEDERS FOR WOODWORKERS, Scott D. Campbell. Detailed, simple-to-use guide for designing, constructing, caring for and using feeders. Text, illustrations for 12 classic and contemporary designs. 96pp. 5⅜ x 8½.
25847-5 Pa. $3.95

SCOTTISH WONDER TALES FROM MYTH AND LEGEND, Donald A. Mackenzie. 16 lively tales tell of giants rumbling down mountainsides, of a magic wand that turns stone pillars into warriors, of gods and goddesses, evil hags, powerful forces and more. 240pp. 5⅜ x 8½. 29677-6 Pa. $6.95

THE HISTORY OF UNDERCLOTHES, C. Willett Cunnington and Phyllis Cunnington. Fascinating, well-documented survey covering six centuries of English undergarments, enhanced with over 100 illustrations: 12th-century laced-up bodice, footed long drawers (1795), 19th-century bustles, 19th-century corsets for men, Victorian "bust improvers," much more. 272pp. 5⅜ x 8¼. 27124-2 Pa. $9.95

ARTS AND CRAFTS FURNITURE: The Complete Brooks Catalog of 1912, Brooks Manufacturing Co. Photos and detailed descriptions of more than 150 now very collectible furniture designs from the Arts and Crafts movement depict davenports, settees, buffets, desks, tables, chairs, bedsteads, dressers and more, all built of solid, quarter-sawed oak. Invaluable for students and enthusiasts of antiques, Americana and the decorative arts. 80pp. 6½ x 9¼. 27471-3 Pa. $8.95

WILBUR AND ORVILLE: A Biography of the Wright Brothers, Fred Howard. Definitive, crisply written study tells the full story of the brothers' lives and work. A vividly written biography, unparalleled in scope and color, that also captures the spirit of an extraordinary era. 560pp. 6⅛ x 9¼. 40297-5 Pa. $17.95

THE ARTS OF THE SAILOR: Knotting, Splicing and Ropework, Hervey Garrett Smith. Indispensable shipboard reference covers tools, basic knots and useful hitches; handsewing and canvas work, more. Over 100 illustrations. Delightful reading for sea lovers. 256pp. 5⅜ x 8½. 26440-8 Pa. $8.95

FRANK LLOYD WRIGHT'S FALLINGWATER: The House and Its History, Second, Revised Edition, Donald Hoffmann. A total revision–both in text and illustrations–of the standard document on Fallingwater, the boldest, most personal architectural statement of Wright's mature years, updated with valuable new material from the recently opened Frank Lloyd Wright Archives. "Fascinating"–*The New York Times*. 116 illustrations. 128pp. 9¼ x 10¾. 27430-6 Pa. $12.95

CATALOG OF DOVER BOOKS

PHOTOGRAPHIC SKETCHBOOK OF THE CIVIL WAR, Alexander Gardner. 100 photos taken on field during the Civil War. Famous shots of Manassas Harper's Ferry, Lincoln, Richmond, slave pens, etc. 244pp. 10⅝ x 8¼. 22731-6 Pa. $10.95

FIVE ACRES AND INDEPENDENCE, Maurice G. Kains. Great back-to-the-land classic explains basics of self-sufficient farming. The one book to get. 95 illustrations. 397pp. 5⅜ x 8½. 20974-1 Pa. $7.95

SONGS OF EASTERN BIRDS, Dr. Donald J. Borror. Songs and calls of 60 species most common to eastern U.S.: warblers, woodpeckers, flycatchers, thrushes, larks, many more in high-quality recording. Cassette and manual 99912-2 $9.95

A MODERN HERBAL, Margaret Grieve. Much the fullest, most exact, most useful compilation of herbal material. Gigantic alphabetical encyclopedia, from aconite to zedoary, gives botanical information, medical properties, folklore, economic uses, much else. Indispensable to serious reader. 161 illustrations. 888pp. 6½ x 9¼. 2-vol. set. (Available in U.S. only.) Vol. I: 22798-7 Pa. $10.95
Vol. II: 22799-5 Pa. $10.95

HIDDEN TREASURE MAZE BOOK, Dave Phillips. Solve 34 challenging mazes accompanied by heroic tales of adventure. Evil dragons, people-eating plants, blood-thirsty giants, many more dangerous adversaries lurk at every twist and turn. 34 mazes, stories, solutions. 48pp. 8¼ x 11. 24566-7 Pa. $2.95

LETTERS OF W. A. MOZART, Wolfgang A. Mozart. Remarkable letters show bawdy wit, humor, imagination, musical insights, contemporary musical world; includes some letters from Leopold Mozart. 276pp. 5⅜ x 8½. 22859-2 Pa. $9.95

BASIC PRINCIPLES OF CLASSICAL BALLET, Agrippina Vaganova. Great Russian theoretician, teacher explains methods for teaching classical ballet. 118 illustrations. 175pp. 5⅜ x 8½. 22036-2 Pa. $6.95

THE JUMPING FROG, Mark Twain. Revenge edition. The original story of The Celebrated Jumping Frog of Calaveras County, a hapless French translation, and Twain's hilarious "retranslation" from the French. 12 illustrations. 66pp. 5⅜ x 8½. 22686-7 Pa. $4.95

BEST REMEMBERED POEMS, Martin Gardner (ed.). The 126 poems in this superb collection of 19th- and 20th-century British and American verse range from Shelley's "To a Skylark" to the impassioned "Renascence" of Edna St. Vincent Millay and to Edward Lear's whimsical "The Owl and the Pussycat." 224pp. 5⅜ x 8½. 27165-X Pa. $5.95

COMPLETE SONNETS, William Shakespeare. Over 150 exquisite poems deal with love, friendship, the tyranny of time, beauty's evanescence, death and other themes in language of remarkable power, precision and beauty. Glossary of archaic terms. 80pp. 5$\frac{3}{16}$ x 8¼. 26686-9 Pa. $1.00

THE BATTLES THAT CHANGED HISTORY, Fletcher Pratt. Eminent historian profiles 16 crucial conflicts, ancient to modern, that changed the course of civilization. 352pp. 5⅜ x 8½. 41129-X Pa. $9.95

THE WIT AND HUMOR OF OSCAR WILDE, Alvin Redman (ed.). More than 1,000 ripostes, paradoxes, wisecracks: Work is the curse of the drinking classes; I can resist everything except temptation; etc. 258pp. 5⅜ x 8½. 20602-5 Pa. $6.95

SHAKESPEARE LEXICON AND QUOTATION DICTIONARY, Alexander Schmidt. Full definitions, locations, shades of meaning in every word in plays and poems. More than 50,000 exact quotations. 1,485pp. 6½ x 9¼. 2-vol. set.
Vol. 1: 22726-X Pa. $17.95
Vol. 2: 22727-8 Pa. $17.95

SELECTED POEMS, Emily Dickinson. Over 100 best-known, best-loved poems by one of America's foremost poets, reprinted from authoritative early editions. No comparable edition at this price. Index of first lines. 64pp. 5³⁄₁₆ x 8¼.
26466-1 Pa. $1.00

THE INSIDIOUS DR. FU-MANCHU, Sax Rohmer. The first of the popular mystery series introduces a pair of English detectives to their archnemesis, the diabolical Dr. Fu-Manchu. Flavorful atmosphere, fast-paced action, and colorful characters enliven this classic of the genre. 208pp. 5³⁄₁₆ x 8¼. 29898-1 Pa. $2.00

THE MALLEUS MALEFICARUM OF KRAMER AND SPRENGER, translated by Montague Summers. Full text of most important witchhunter's "bible," used by both Catholics and Protestants. 278pp. 6⅝ x 10. 22802-9 Pa. $12.95

SPANISH STORIES/CUENTOS ESPAÑOLES: A Dual-Language Book, Angel Flores (ed.). Unique format offers 13 great stories in Spanish by Cervantes, Borges, others. Faithful English translations on facing pages. 352pp. 5⅜ x 8½.
25399-6 Pa. $9.95

GARDEN CITY, LONG ISLAND, IN EARLY PHOTOGRAPHS, 1869–1919, Mildred H. Smith. Handsome treasury of 118 vintage pictures, accompanied by carefully researched captions, document the Garden City Hotel fire (1899), the Vanderbilt Cup Race (1908), the first airmail flight departing from the Nassau Boulevard Aerodrome (1911), and much more. 96pp. 8⅞ x 11¾. 40669-5 Pa. $12.95

OLD QUEENS, N.Y., IN EARLY PHOTOGRAPHS, Vincent F. Seyfried and William Asadorian. Over 160 rare photographs of Maspeth, Jamaica, Jackson Heights, and other areas. Vintage views of DeWitt Clinton mansion, 1939 World's Fair and more. Captions. 192pp. 8⅞ x 11. 26358-4 Pa. $14.95

CAPTURED BY THE INDIANS: 15 Firsthand Accounts, 1750-1870, Frederick Drimmer. Astounding true historical accounts of grisly torture, bloody conflicts, relentless pursuits, miraculous escapes and more, by people who lived to tell the tale. 384pp. 5⅜ x 8½. 24901-8 Pa. $9.95

THE WORLD'S GREAT SPEECHES (Fourth Enlarged Edition), Lewis Copeland, Lawrence W. Lamm, and Stephen J. McKenna. Nearly 300 speeches provide public speakers with a wealth of updated quotes and inspiration–from Pericles' funeral oration and William Jennings Bryan's "Cross of Gold Speech" to Malcolm X's powerful words on the Black Revolution and Earl of Spenser's tribute to his sister, Diana, Princess of Wales. 944pp. 5⅜ x 8⅜. 40903-1 Pa. $15.95

THE BOOK OF THE SWORD, Sir Richard F. Burton. Great Victorian scholar/adventurer's eloquent, erudite history of the "queen of weapons"–from prehistory to early Roman Empire. Evolution and development of early swords, variations (sabre, broadsword, cutlass, scimitar, etc.), much more. 336pp. 6⅛ x 9¼.
25434-8 Pa. $9.95

AUTOBIOGRAPHY: The Story of My Experiments with Truth, Mohandas K. Gandhi. Boyhood, legal studies, purification, the growth of the Satyagraha (nonviolent protest) movement. Critical, inspiring work of the man responsible for the freedom of India. 480pp. 5⅜ x 8½. (Available in U.S. only.)   24593-4 Pa. $9.95

CELTIC MYTHS AND LEGENDS, T. W. Rolleston. Masterful retelling of Irish and Welsh stories and tales. Cuchulain, King Arthur, Deirdre, the Grail, many more. First paperback edition. 58 full-page illustrations. 512pp. 5⅜ x 8½.   26507-2 Pa. $9.95

THE PRINCIPLES OF PSYCHOLOGY, William James. Famous long course complete, unabridged. Stream of thought, time perception, memory, experimental methods; great work decades ahead of its time. 94 figures. 1,391pp. 5⅜ x 8½. 2-vol. set.
Vol. I: 20381-6 Pa. $14.95
Vol. II: 20382-4 Pa. $16.95

THE WORLD AS WILL AND REPRESENTATION, Arthur Schopenhauer. Definitive English translation of Schopenhauer's life work, correcting more than 1,000 errors, omissions in earlier translations. Translated by E. F. J. Payne. Total of 1,269pp. 5⅜ x 8½. 2-vol. set.
Vol. 1: 21761-2 Pa. $12.95
Vol. 2: 21762-0 Pa. $12.95

MAGIC AND MYSTERY IN TIBET, Madame Alexandra David-Neel. Experiences among lamas, magicians, sages, sorcerers, Bonpa wizards. A true psychic discovery. 32 illustrations. 321pp. 5⅜ x 8½. (Available in U.S. only.)   22682-4 Pa. $9.95

THE EGYPTIAN BOOK OF THE DEAD, E. A. Wallis Budge. Complete reproduction of Ani's papyrus, finest ever found. Full hieroglyphic text, interlinear transliteration, word-for-word translation, smooth translation. 533pp. 6½ x 9¼.
21866-X Pa. $12.95

MATHEMATICS FOR THE NONMATHEMATICIAN, Morris Kline. Detailed, college-level treatment of mathematics in cultural and historical context, with numerous exercises. Recommended Reading Lists. Tables. Numerous figures. 641pp. 5⅜ x 8½.
24823-2 Pa. $11.95

PROBABILISTIC METHODS IN THE THEORY OF STRUCTURES, Isaac Elishakoff. Well-written introduction covers the elements of the theory of probability from two or more random variables, the reliability of such multivariable structures, the theory of random function, Monte Carlo methods of treating problems incapable of exact solution, and more. Examples. 502pp. 5³⁄₈ x 8¹⁄₂.   40691-1 Pa. $16.95

THE RIME OF THE ANCIENT MARINER, Gustave Doré, S. T. Coleridge. Doré's finest work; 34 plates capture moods, subtleties of poem. Flawless full-size reproductions printed on facing pages with authoritative text of poem. "Beautiful. Simply beautiful."–*Publisher's Weekly.* 77pp. 9¼ x 12.   22305-1 Pa. $7.95

NORTH AMERICAN INDIAN DESIGNS FOR ARTISTS AND CRAFTSPEOPLE, Eva Wilson. Over 360 authentic copyright-free designs adapted from Navajo blankets, Hopi pottery, Sioux buffalo hides, more. Geometrics, symbolic figures, plant and animal motifs, etc. 128pp. 8⅜ x 11. (Not for sale in the United Kingdom.)   25341-4 Pa. $9.95

SCULPTURE: Principles and Practice, Louis Slobodkin. Step-by-step approach to clay, plaster, metals, stone; classical and modern. 253 drawings, photos. 255pp. 8⅛ x 11.
22960-2 Pa. $11.95

THE INFLUENCE OF SEA POWER UPON HISTORY, 1660–1783, A. T. Mahan. Influential classic of naval history and tactics still used as text in war colleges. First paperback edition. 4 maps. 24 battle plans. 640pp. 5⅜ x 8½.   25509-3 Pa. $14.95

THE STORY OF THE TITANIC AS TOLD BY ITS SURVIVORS, Jack Winocour (ed.). What it was really like. Panic, despair, shocking inefficiency, and a little heroism. More thrilling than any fictional account. 26 illustrations. 320pp. 5⅜ x 8½.
20610-6 Pa. $8.95

FAIRY AND FOLK TALES OF THE IRISH PEASANTRY, William Butler Yeats (ed.). Treasury of 64 tales from the twilight world of Celtic myth and legend: "The Soul Cages," "The Kildare Pooka," "King O'Toole and his Goose," many more. Introduction and Notes by W. B. Yeats. 352pp. 5⅜ x 8½.   26941-8 Pa. $8.95

BUDDHIST MAHAYANA TEXTS, E. B. Cowell and others (eds.). Superb, accurate translations of basic documents in Mahayana Buddhism, highly important in history of religions. The Buddha-karita of Asvaghosha, Larger Sukhavativyuha, more. 448pp. 5⅜ x 8½.   25552-2 Pa. $12.95

ONE TWO THREE . . . INFINITY: Facts and Speculations of Science, George Gamow. Great physicist's fascinating, readable overview of contemporary science: number theory, relativity, fourth dimension, entropy, genes, atomic structure, much more. 128 illustrations. Index. 352pp. 5⅜ x 8½.   25664-2 Pa. $9.95

EXPERIMENTATION AND MEASUREMENT, W. J. Youden. Introductory manual explains laws of measurement in simple terms and offers tips for achieving accuracy and minimizing errors. Mathematics of measurement, use of instruments, experimenting with machines. 1994 edition. Foreword. Preface. Introduction. Epilogue. Selected Readings. Glossary. Index. Tables and figures. 128pp. $5^{3}/_{8}$ x $8^{1}/_{2}$.
40451-X Pa. $6.95

DALÍ ON MODERN ART: The Cuckolds of Antiquated Modern Art, Salvador Dalí. Influential painter skewers modern art and its practitioners. Outrageous evaluations of Picasso, Cézanne, Turner, more. 15 renderings of paintings discussed. 44 calligraphic decorations by Dalí. 96pp. 5⅜ x 8½. (Available in U.S. only.)   29220-7 Pa. $5.95

ANTIQUE PLAYING CARDS: A Pictorial History, Henry René D'Allemagne. Over 900 elaborate, decorative images from rare playing cards (14th–20th centuries): Bacchus, death, dancing dogs, hunting scenes, royal coats of arms, players cheating, much more. 96pp. 9¼ x 12¼.   29265-7 Pa. $12.95

MAKING FURNITURE MASTERPIECES: 30 Projects with Measured Drawings, Franklin H. Gottshall. Step-by-step instructions, illustrations for constructing handsome, useful pieces, among them a Sheraton desk, Chippendale chair, Spanish desk, Queen Anne table and a William and Mary dressing mirror. 224pp. 8⅛ x 11¼.
29338-6 Pa. $16.95

THE FOSSIL BOOK: A Record of Prehistoric Life, Patricia V. Rich et al. Profusely illustrated definitive guide covers everything from single-celled organisms and dinosaurs to birds and mammals and the interplay between climate and man. Over 1,500 illustrations. 760pp. 7½ x 10⅛.   29371-8 Pa. $29.95

Prices subject to change without notice.